Cruising Across America!

Carey Masci

Copyright © 2018 by Carey Masci

Cruising Across America!

Carey Masci, Author

Michael T. Petro, Jr., Editor

Published by Petro Publications
Cleveland, Ohio USA
PetroPublications.com

Front & Back Cover © by Carey Masci

All Photographs Copyright © by Carey Masci

ISBN-10: 0-9650411-8-2

ISBN-13: 978-0-9650411-8-8

Dedication

Inspiration comes from within and from those whom God places in your life. So, I dedicate this book to everyone mentioned in it. After all, they were all part of my life's adventure.

And also to Dad Kelly! The first time I met him I was welcomed into his house. We sat around his kitchen table conversing for hours. He told me story after interesting story of his life. Kelly inspired me so much that I thought to myself "Someday I will have more experiences than him." That's how much his stories challenged me to go out and experience all that life has to offer.

Table of Contents

Preface..VII

Chapter One: Strange Place to Eat.................................1

Chapter Two: What to Pack and Some Travel Tips........................2

Chapter Three: Instant Friends...................................6

Chapter Four: Here's Another Example
of an Instant Friend Helped by a Careyism....................11

Chapter Five: Where Were You When the Moon Went Dim?...16

Chapter Six: Directions to Where I Live............................32

Chapter Seven: To Hell and Back..................................34

Chapter Eight: The Shower..43

Chapter Nine: Christmas Events Ohio-Style..................44

Chapter Ten: A Christmas Memory..............................47

Chapter Eleven: Anything Open?..................................48

Chapter Twelve: Fall Festival Summer Fun...................49

Chapter Thirteen: Cherry Springs State Park................52

Chapter Fourteen: Turf and Surf or Soup? 63

Chapter Fifteen: Letchworth and Our Heaven-Sent Angels........64

Chapter Sixteen: Night and Day....................................73

Chapter Seventeen: Mansfield Reformatory Trip...........74

Chapter Eighteen: Pace Yourself...................................82

Chapter Nineteen: Morning Revenge.............................83

Chapter Twenty: Notes from the
Trip to Butch Holler, Kentucky.....................................84

Chapter Twenty-One: Greenville
and the Tionesta Breakdown..87

Closing Remarks..103

Preface

Hey Gang!

My first book titled *Hey Gang! Ready to Go-Go?* was warmly greeted, and when the majority of the people I met at book signings read the title they responded with "I am always ready to go-go."

Well then, with that I say, "Hey Gang! Let's Go-Go!"

And for those of you who did buy the first book, you may recall a few paragraphs of this Preface as I borrowed from it, rather than reinventing the wheel. But besides repeating those few paragraphs, all of the stories are new.

And if you haven't bought the first book, put this one down and go buy it. Not that it matters, but you do want to be able to say "I got the complete set," don't you?

What is the Premise of this Book?

Like the previous book, this one is also travel-related, but not in the traditional sense. It's a light-hearted, fun look at the great American road trip by way of my amusing and entertaining travel experiences, adventures, misadventures, gaffes and laughs.

Some chapters are written in story form, other chapters are just notes and highlights. Through listening to feedback about the first book I have included a few stories that are much longer in nature, covering trips from start to finish. So for those who wondered what it would be like to be a passenger on one of my adventures can travel right along for the entire journey.

Are All These Stories True?

Yes, all these stories are true, and the people mentioned are real. In the first draft of the first book, *Hey Gang! Ready to Go-Go?* I had "friend" written over and over to the point of redundancy. So, I rewrote it and, if the story really had little to do with who I was with, their name was omitted. Sorry! But, if a friend or acquaintance is part or a focal point in the story, their name is included. I have continued on with this in *Cruising Across America!* After all, how could I use fictitious names because these books were written with you in mind and you just may find "you" in them?

And just like book one, the fun stories contained between the covers here also have a useful side. If you want to take notes of places or sites mentioned, you could use it as a travel guide and visit them yourself.

Why did I write this book?

I still had plenty of material left over after I finished the first book, so I decided a second book was needed to cover my many road trip experiences. Blame my editor, he is the one who wouldn't allow me to cram any more into the first book. And if you want to know why I wrote the first book you will have to read it because I tell you why.

Besides, I had so much fun with my first book it just beckoned to be followed up with another.

How fun was it?

I am a "people person," and the opportunity of meeting interesting people and making new friends at book signings is great!

It's a wonderful feeling having someone approach me saying they enjoyed my book, and then relaying to me their travel experiences, their family road trips, or things they remembered from years past.

Of course, it made me feel equally as good when they said "I loved your bathroom incident story." And it really warms my heart that people all over now know about the spinning spatula. Ah yes, that makes me feel grand!

Not all reviews were positive, like the individual who told me it was "Eh, OK," but then proceeded to talk my ear off. He told me story after story of his family vacations of when he was a boy and later on as a parent. When he was done I felt like I heard another version of *Hey Gang!* But he didn't like my book. Oh well!

Besides making new friends, I learned quite a lot at book signings. Here are just two of the important lessons I learned that may help those who wish to venture into writing their own book someday.

Lesson One

<u>Slow Down and Don't Be Overly Confident</u>

The Go-Go Bus had some work done at Tuffy Auto Services Center in Mentor, Ohio. When I went to pick it up I brought in a copy of *Hey Gang!* and said to Ron the owner, "You need this book, so how would you like me to sign it?" He replied, "Tuffy would be good." I grabbed a pen and he questioned me by saying "You sure you want to use a pen, what happens if you make a mistake?"

I replied "I've been to many book signings, I won't make a mistake." Well, he must have put the whammy on me because I misspelled "Bus." I wrote it with two S's.

To make matters worse, I thought it was an eraser at the other end of his pen. It wasn't. The rubber tip only smeared what I wrote. He said, "Leave it alone. I'll take the book as is." I left the book, but dang did I feel stupid and embarrassed!

Lesson Two

<u>Have an Arsenal of Pens Ready in Case One Won't Write</u>

Ah yes, make sure you have backup pens available. On one occasion I sold the last book I had to a couple. Right in the middle of signing it the pen ran out of ink. I was upset and told the husband and wife "I am sorry, this is a family book and there is just no way I can give you this copy. My pen stopped writing. You are not getting this copy."

Reluctantly, I showed them what was written before the pen went on vacation. It read "Marc and Emily, Pleasure me." Sorry, but no one is going to see my book with those words. Just in time Ruth, who was in standby, found a pen in her purse and came to the rescue. I finished signing the book. It was in different colored ink, but it passed censorship.

It now reads "Marc and Emily, Pleasure meeting you."

So, I hope that you will find *Cruising Across America!* as entertaining as *Hey Gang! Ready to Go-Go?* I also hope it will encourage you to go out and enjoy this great land of ours called America.

Now, are you ready to get started? Well then if you are, fill your travel mug and...*Let's Go Cruising Across America!*

Chapter One

Strange Place to Eat

(Since this second book is following the path of the first book, and that one started with breakfast, so why not start with breakfast again!)

One of the strangest places I ever ate at was the Weirton Restaurant Cab Company in West Virginia; I believe that was the name of it. The place looked condemned from the outside and inside not much better, but the breakfast was actually pretty good.

When I entered I took a seat at the counter. The chair I grabbed had a bent leg and was leaning quite badly. I told the cook "I better grab a different chair, you're starting to look slanted." He said "I've been told that before." I switched chairs, sat down, looked up and that's when I realized he was severely hunched with one leg considerably shorter than the other. Boy oh boy, did I feel bad with my off the wall comment!

As the cook was making my breakfast the phone rang. He answered it, took directions and said, "We will send a cab right over." That's when it occurred to me the place was not only a restaurant but also a cab company – and the cook was also the dispatcher!

My eggs were delivered on time, and I am sure the cab was also.

Chapter Two

What to Pack and Some Travel Tips

I used to carry milk when I traveled. It took up space in the cooler or fridge and many times it soured. I now carry packets or a small container of powdered milk. It's just as good, saves space and doesn't spoil.

Another neat tip is to freeze your bottled water before you go. The bottles act as ice for the other foods you carry, plus you will have ice-cold water to sip as it thaws.

Have You Ever Forgotten a Pan?

This happened on two separate camping occasions.

One time I brought steaks to cook. We not only forgot a pan but also a rack for the fire pit. So I went down to the river, found a flat rock, washed it off, heated it up real good, then threw our steaks on it. Walt still says it was the best steak he ever ate. This was way before the restaurant that cooks their steaks on a stone. Who knows, maybe they copied me!

Another time without a pan I wanted to make eggs for breakfast. What to do, what to do? A beer can, I mean a pop can. I chopped the can in half, dropped an egg into it then set it on the fire. An egg fits perfectly, but just make sure you have some butter, or use cooking oil, or the egg will stick. Everyone knows there's nothing worse than a sticky egg!

Pine Needles

One of the best fire starters are dried pine needles. I can usually start a fire with pine needles just about as fast as when using lighter fluid. When you're camping or at a cookout find a pine tree. Lift up the bottom branches and you will find a bounty of needles. Scoop up a couple of handfuls.

First line the grill or fire pit with crumpled paper, on top of that the dried needles, next kindling and then light. It should catch almost instantly.

Baby Powder

I always carry baby powder. For those who think it's not manly enough, well then make it talcum powder. I always carry talcum powder. And before you think otherwise it's not because I wet myself but to keep myself dry. It is a must when I travel to have powder. At the end of a hike or any outdoor activity I put it in my shoes or boots to dry them; I use powder on a wash cloth and dry and freshen myself, and when water is not available to wash clothes. Powder is a great way to dry clean clothes. I put my hands in my socks, sprinkle powder on them, rub together, turn them inside out and do it again. It dries, cleans and takes away odor. You can use this on other articles of clothing as well.

Tarp

Always carry a tarp. Yes a tarp, not to be confused with carp or harp – tarp. A large tarp! Carry one. Carry one at least 10'X15'. I have used tarps to cover a picnic table when an abrupt rainfall moves in; used it to line the ground before putting up a tent; used it over my car and set it up like a tent to sleep under (Yes, I have!), and over the Go-Go Bus for added shade and to keep rain out when I have the windows open. You could also use bungee cords and string up a tarp between trees like a canopy.

Soap Up Before

Another little trick I use when no facilities are available to wash is this: I lather up with liquid soap and jump in a pond, river, or lake. I know what you are thinking, this causes pollution. Well then use bio-degradable soap. Besides, do you know how many people use the beach and have suntan lotion on, deodorant, perfume, hair gel, or spray, and use it to, well you know? So my little bit of soap, I feel, is no big thing.

Anyway... just make sure a beach is at hand or you don't mind paying if one charges a fee. My nephew Seth still talks about the time I took him camping around the Rocky Fork area in Ohio. I told him of my bright idea of how to soap up. He was hesitant until I told him we are driving immediately down to the beach. We lather up real good, extra good, leave our campground and head to the beach only to be greeted by a toll booth with a woman asking for a fee. There was positively no way I was going to pay just to rinse off. Boy of boy, was my nephew upset and itchy, very itchy! So was I, but I wasn't going to complain about myself.

An hour plus later still driving around in the heat with soap dried on us and our hair all sticky I finally found another beach that didn't charge. We got clean but my nephew, well, he hasn't forgotten about this bright idea.

Chapter Three

Instant Friends

We had breakfast, I gave you some tips on what to bring, now let's meet some of my "instant friends!"

Dad always had a passion for traveling and road trips. He preferred the less traveled roads and particularly liked night travel. There were many nights when dad would spontaneously say "Let's go for a ride" and the family would pile into the car. Sitting in the backseat as a child looking out at the changing scenery and houses on those trips, I would often wonder who lived in them, what kind of people they were, what did the inside of their dwellings look like? Night travel only increased my curiosity, especially way out in the country where the intrigue of the darkness was broken by an occasional farmhouse with lights on.

Little did I know years later my curiosity would be answered as I have been blessed with meeting people and being invited into their homes. Many times all it took for that invite to happen was a hand shake or a smile, which was usually followed with, "Well, come on in!"

Here are a few of those instant friends I made while out on the road, and as you continue reading this book you will meet even more.

Ed

I met Ed while trespassing on his property and didn't even know it. I was driving through Cameron, West Virginia with friends when we spotted an abandoned house. I pulled off the side of the road and all of us went to investigate. Once inside someone started yelling. Thinking we may get shot, one friend ran out the back door, another jumped from a window and hid in the woods, and I, acting on sheer bravery, made my girlfriend go see what the man wanted. Instead of shooting, he was just wondering what we were doing in that house. When the "All's safe" signal was given by my girlfriend, I sheepishly came out the front door, 30 came from behind the house, and Jamie, well, we had to repeatedly yell to him "It's OK, you can come out now!" After formal introductions were made and we became convinced we would not be shot, we went to Ed's house for coffee. How good was the coffee and the hospitality from Ed and his family? We ended up staying for three days.

Wilf & Joyce

People talk about southern hospitality, but let's not forget about Canadian hospitality.

I was in one of my "Hey, what are you doing? Want to go on a road trip?" moods when the idea of Niagara Falls came into mind. "Hello Dennis, want to go?" And just like that there we were at the falls. After viewing the falls I thought it would be neat for reminiscing sake to find my Aunt and Uncles old house that I remember staying at as a child. I found it but I got lost on the return.

Dennis and I were going back and forth on what to do when I spotted two couples standing in front of a house. I said, "I am just going to pull in and ask." Dennis was quick to say "NO, don't do that, you're not going to pull in someone's drive you don't know." "OH YEAH!" He should know never to say "No" to me. So I pulled into this driveway and ask loudly "Excuse me, we're lost. Which way to the falls?" Of course they had to come over to see what I was driving, and I had to get out to look at their garden and huge sunflowers. Their names were Wilf and Joyce, daughter Elaine and son-in-law Art. After introductions and a garden tour, I was invited to a "Cruise in" on Bundy's Lane where Elaine and Art were headed. Before leaving, Wilf and Joyce offered us the use of their driveway to park for the night if we needed a place to sleep. We attended the car show and later on went back and accepted the driveway invite. In the morning Wilf and Joyce welcomed us in for breakfast. I was fascinated by Wilf's skill at gardening and woodworking. In his kitchen is a hutch he built from a tree he planted many years before on his property. Canadian hospitality, you bet!

Emerson

Good ole Emerson Babbington, what a character!

We were winding our way through the countryside of southern Ohio, heading northwest, when we came upon the abandoned McCoppin Mill on Rocky Fork Lake. It has since been torched by an arsonist and no longer standing. This is also when I met Emerson, or shall I say he met me. Denise, Seth and I went to explore the mill when a car pulled up to chase us out. Before this man could say anything more than "What are you doing here?" I grabbed a piece of paper that was on the ground and said "I saw this and was wondering what it was since I collect old things." The grounds of the mill were somewhat neglected with old junk lying around. From there I started asking more and more questions to keep myself out of trouble and Emerson distracted from the reason why he stopped.

Then Emerson took the floor and told me he was just 19 years old when he got stranded and made this area his home. How that happened was his car battery died, and having no money for a new one, he stayed. Two years later he bought land and made this his permanent residence. Because of the beauty, Emerson nicknamed this area "God's Country," which many people now refer to it as. From there Emerson told the audience of one, me, how he used to spar, when he got saved, about his campground, and about a dozen other events and happenings from his life.

Emerson talked so long that he never noticed that Denise and Seth continued on with their exploration of the mill, which was supposed to be off limits. Directly after the mill we went to Babbington's campground and stayed for two days. I could go on and on with Emerson stories, the man who eats coffee grounds and serves fungus from trees on bread.

Good ole Emerson Babbington, what a character, and even better friend!

Chapter Four

Here's Another Example of an Instant Friend Helped by a Careyism

(Careyism? Read my first book, you'll understand!)

My friend Joe contacted me to ask if I could assist his disabled friend Chris in Akron to get to his father's funeral in Indiana. As instructed by Joe, I called the gentleman who needed a ride. I was at my rental house when this phone conversation took place.

We exchanged names but I didn't understand his last name. Chris said "Durham." I asked "How do you spell it?" He replied "As in Durham, North Carolina." "How do you spell that? I am not familiar with Durham, North Carolina." He spelled out "Durham," slowly.

After the call ended I resumed my cleaning and clearing out junk from the last tenant who just vacated, and sitting on the TV wall unit was a baseball card that was left behind. The name of the player on the card was – Ray Durham!

I immediately called Chris back and asked "What is your father's name again?" Chris replied "Ray Durham." I said "You won't believe this but my tenant who just moved out left sitting on a shelf a baseball card. And the players name is, ready for this? Ray Durham of the San Francisco Giants! RAY DURHAM, the same name as your father's name, RAY DURHAM. This is just plain spooky! What are the chances of finding a baseball card with the same name of someone you were just talking about?" To this day I am still amazed by this! Anyway, after our bafflement subsided we exchanged emails and I gave him the link to my book. Chris said, "Well, maybe you can write about our trip to Indiana and I can receive royalties." I replied, "I am ahead of you, I already wrote notes down, but I am not so sure about the royalties though."

So with such a start to a friendship as that, finding a baseball card with the same name of Chris's father, how could I not include Chris in my book? And of course, I decided to drive him to Indiana.

Onward to Richmond, Indiana

The vehicle Chris rented is called a MV1. What a neat vehicle! It is made solely for wheelchairs.

It weighs 6,000 pounds, but the lady at the rental office said be careful of the brakes, they stop on a dime. I forgot that warning and almost made Chris pop out of his wheelchair the first couple of stops.

Anyway, Chris is enjoyable to travel with and says he is having a great trip. Unfortunately it had to be to attend his father's funeral.

We stopped at a truck stop called the Iron Skillet Restaurant in New Paris, Ohio, almost on the state line of Indiana. It's a typical old-style truck stop, though I was informed a corporation bought them out, and usually when that happens things change, and not for the better.

Our waiter said he works three jobs, all in the restaurant field. He was interesting. He has been to six states helping to start up restaurants in New Jersey, Pennsylvania, Kentucky, Ohio, Mississippi, and North Dakota. He told me that in North Dakota there are so many Somalis and Albanians it was crazy. They refuse to work and would rather collect government benefits. Golden Corral decided to shut down, not because of no business, but because they couldn't find people willing to work. And so it is in, "Global America!"

We are now at the hotel and I best sleep as the wake and funeral starts at 10:00 a.m. If I don't sleep they may bury me.

Memoriam for Bruce

My thoughts and feelings bounce around quite a bit trying to write about the funeral. It was beyond strange this whole trip. Chris was easy to converse with and I almost lost sight of the real meaning of why I was there. When we got to the funeral home for the visitation and wake I wasn't sure if I should leave or stay. I was hired to drive Chris, but in 24 hours I got to know him and I felt maybe I should stay – almost like a friend. Chris told me he wanted me to stay to hear the eulogy for his dad.

I stayed at the visitation for a while then left and took a short drive. Indiana is a very homey state. Many sections of it have small rural towns that seem lost in time. After a brief look around I returned and napped in the car. My nap ran over so I missed the minister, but I did hear what Bruce's friends and Chris had to say about the deceased. You can learn a lot about a person by what people and friends say. They all had high praises for Bruce, so much so that I wish I could have met him. From what I gather he must have been a bit wild when younger, but came to know the Lord and really turned his life around. He was a genuine, caring, loving, family man and one terrific guitarist. The band he played for backed up Mickey Gilley.

I sat back and reflected during the funeral. This is what came to mind: One: All families are the same. Two: Life is short. Three: Without God life is meaningless. Four: How many Bruce's are out there that we just didn't reach out and meet?

I must thank Chris and his family and friends for welcoming me in as part of their family during this trying time. I want them to know that they are in my prayers and are all special.

This is What Chris Spoke During the Wake

"My message at my father's, Bruce Durham's, funeral.

"I want to talk with you today about something that touches all of us.....Loss!

"Sometimes we are faced with things we think we just can't handle and we strive to find the meaning behind it all. And when we can't do that, often we look up and say 'God, how could you do this to us? How could you put so much on our plate?' But we are not operating on God's timetable. We don't understand God's plan. How can we? Let me tell you, this is where faith comes in. Faith is the substance of things unseen. And with my father, he wanted us all to see the things that are often unseen. And that is the same faith that will allow us to send dad home. Faith is there to show us his message in our own lives from today forward; to share that hope and faith; to love others as bravely and as fiercely as we can. Loss teaches us to not take anything for granted. And from loss comes love, forgiving, relentless and unconditional love. In that love, you will find peace.

In Ecclesiastes, which dad discussed with me on our last visit together, I find these words are most likely the ones dad wants me to share:

"I have seen what is best for people to do on Earth: They should eat, drink, and enjoy the work they have during their short time here. God has given them these few days, and that is all they have. If God gives some people wealth, property, and the power to enjoy those things, they should enjoy them. They should accept the things they have and enjoy their work; that is a gift from God! People don't have many years to live, so they must remember these things all their lives. God will keep them busy with the work they love to do."

Ray was known by family and friends as Bruce, his middle name.

Chapter Five

Where Were You
When The Moon Went Dim?

This is my story of the trip to see the great eclipse of 2017. What a whirlwind road trip of four days it was! We had an Ark Encounter, almost encountered my friend Mike, never encounter-ed Janet, but Ruth had an encounter with Karen, who countered with "Follow me, you can park the night at my place, there is nothing around, you can roam the property. You do have a flash light – right?"

It was Janet's idea to see the eclipse somewhere in Tennessee at a place called Rock Island State Park, which I never heard of. About a week before leaving is when Ruth and I finally decided to tag along with Janet and her family, but we would be leaving a day early and try to catch up with them on the road. Try is the keyword here. We left early so we could stop in Williamstown, Kentucky to tour the Noah's Ark replica.

I didn't take any directions other than to the ark. I figured Janet would eventually call and direct us where to meet them. We would tour the ark, then head south and find Janet. Its all that I planned, simple as most of my trips are planned; they only get a bit complicated or stressful when I get lost, well sort of, but not really, well maybe!

I was very anxious and curious to see the ark, or the Ark Encounter, as it is called. It definitely didn't disappoint; it exceeded my expectations. Once you see the ark replica and read their explanations of events surrounding the flood and after, it all makes sense. Viewing it can really bolster your faith or make you think long and hard on your beliefs.

One thing we should have planned better though was viewing it. It's a long tour that is self-guided and if you watch the movies set up on screens, read all the descriptions and see all the displays, it can take up to four hours. We took three and one-half.

We should have seen half, taken a break, ate at the buffet on the grounds, then finished the tour. We left in awe of what we saw. Its well worth the price of admission, with lots to see and a flood of information.

When we first entered the ark my phone rang. It's my friend Mike. "Hey, I just saw your Go-Go Bus in the lot!" What's the chance of running into someone on the road like that? He decided not to tour the ark but it was still fun receiving that call. My thoughts at that time of the phone call were, "Well, if Mike can find me unplanned, then meeting up with Janet and her family should be no problem. She'll call and we'll find them! Yeah, right!"

After the Ark Encounter it was time to head south into Tennessee to find Janet and Rock Island to witness another phenomenon of God – the great eclipse. I was a bit concerned though because Janet had not called yet and I couldn't locate Rock Island on the map. I thought when I briefly looked at it through MapQuest on my home PC it was by Knoxville. Well, I was wrong.

Your thoughts are probably, "Well, why didn't you call Janet?" Simple! I didn't have her cell phone number, and I am sure you are thinking, "Why didn't you use your Smartphone?" Simple! I don't have one. One of the joys of traveling is going carefree, getting lost, worrying where the heck you are, then have it all turn out for the better, as in this trip. C'mon try it, it's fun regardless of what I wrote previously.

We drove Rt. 75 into Tennessee and stopped right over the border at the Tennessee Welcome Center. The buzz and excitement at the center was all about the eclipse. The man behind the counter was talking to people from all over the U.S. In our brief visit I met a family from Pontiac, Michigan.

I asked for directions, but the guy manning it had no clue where Rock Island was and neither did a lady standing next to him. He couldn't find it on the map. Finally, he located it on a brochure for state parks. We were way too far east. "Head west young man," was his advice. He highlighted a map and handed it to us. I shook his hand, thanked him again and left to find Rock Island.

Once I climbed into the Go-Go Bus I decided on taking a different route – the back roads, which I think were shorter. But if you are weary or scared of being in the middle of nowhere on curvy roads at 2:00 a.m., it is not the route for you. I navigated the Go-Go Bus through dark, somewhat foggy mountain roads and arrived close to our destination without incident.

Finding Rock Island State Park was another matter though. We wasted a good hour, maybe more, finding it because of poorly marked signs. When we did arrive the campground had a barricade up with a sign that read PARK OPENS AT 7:00 a.m. A car behind me pulled up and asked if I was lost. He was a local, and said "I am going in, park by the office until they arrive." But instead of waiting where this person told me, we found an empty camp site. We left a note at the office explaining when we pulled in, our vehicle, and the time we would come to the office to pay for the site, even though there was a sign at the office reading "Campground Full."

Around 8:00 a.m. a park ranger pulls up to our site and says "Hello, we got your note but this site is taken. I called around for you and there is a campground nearby that has one site left. "Here's their card; call them ASAP!" How's that for service? I asked if I could sleep a bit longer and he replied "Sure, sleep till noon, they can't sign in until then, so you can stay." With that he drove off, I dozed off, and Ruth took off to take advantage of the showers – all for free! Without tidying up the Go-Go Bus we leave to find the campground with only one site left that the ranger said, "Do it ASAP." But of course that warning to me was not as urgent as more sleep.

Everywhere you went the buzz was about the eclipse. Campgrounds all full, more than average visitors and increased traffic; it was no different at the camp office. So instead of waiting in line I stopped a ranger to ask where this other campground was. The ranger turned out to be the one who woke us. Even with directions I got lost. So I called Collins River Camp, Ramp and RV Park directly and they put me on the right path. Their name sounds like a country and western song, at least to me.

When I saw the campground it was old school, um, make that primitive school. The entrance is a long drive and not the smoothest. "Where's the ramp?" It didn't look like a campground, more like a very small backwoods trailer park. Then we realized it was a mobile home park. The campground was down another rut-filled dirt path. Again, "Where's the ramp?" I can't believe I tortured the poor Go-Go Bus driving down it.

This was a primitive campground alright, for sure not what we expected. It is really suited for tents only, which is what we saw, tents only. I don't know if it even had pit toilets. Maybe it was a carry-in carry-out park? Though I will say if I was tent camping I would love it. Right by the river and shaded, just perfect! And now I know why the word "ramp" is in the title; ramp is for the launching of boats. There was just no way I was staying here. Going in and out with a suitable vehicle is OK, but not with what I was driving.

It was approaching 1:00 p.m., and wanting to see the sites and little shops in town put finding a place to park for tomorrow's big event on the back burner. We were still in hopes Janet would call and we could stay with them, wherever that was.

Rock Island's shops were all closed on Sunday, so we went back to the state park and did some hiking. It is such a beautiful area, with plenty of scenic trails and a beach with large boulders to climb on or jump off of. Some trails are challenging and some have waterfalls. Another place I like to revisit. Our hiking day was done, now what? Where do we park, where's Janet, maybe she would know?

Usually I can park anywhere for the night, but not this time. I spoke with another local ranger/cop who told me "No, you can't do that" when I asked if I can park in the overflow lot for Rock Island. I said "Years ago in Tennessee and Kentucky it was so rural you could have parked anywhere and camped for the night. I know, on a few occasions I ventured off the road and camped with people." He replied "Not anymore, the Health Department won't allow it; you need to be on a site and with facilities."

Rock Island Beach

Health Department? MY OH MY have times changed! I am sure there are spots where you can get away with it, but this was Rock Island's big day for revenue. I saw plenty of tickets written for being illegally parked. I was told to stay away, venture out further for a place to park for the night; it was going to be madness on Monday for the eclipse.

So we left Rock Island, wandered and ended up in the little city of McMinnville, Tennessee, less than 15 miles away. We did some shopping, then it was off to find a local park with a grill to cook. A cop directed us to Pepper Branch, which was perfect.

I circled the park looking for a grill close to where I would park. But in the lot closest to the grills sat two patrol cars with lights on, checking out a car. I wanted to avoid whatever was happening, but I also didn't want to lug everything a good distance, so I chose this area.

As I walked past I was asked "Do you know anything about this?" Did they think my circling the park repeatedly was because I was returning to the scene of the crime? How many people commit crimes in a two-tone purple house-car? I said "No, what happened?" "A car window was smashed and a purse stolen out of it, but we can't find the owner." HUH? Now, that is a true mystery that made no sense. If the owner is missing how did they know a purse was stolen? Hmmm! I still don't know.

While the crime scene was being investigated we made our supper. It was now dusk and still no shower for me, so it was time to take a parking lot shower, then I would worry once again on where to park. How does one take a parking lot shower? Ask me sometime.

After my shower I slipped into fresh clothes when I heard Ruth talking to a lady. I peak my head out as Ruth is telling her what my vehicle was. I said, "Hand her a postcard for my book." From there Ruth explained how we were clueless on where we were going. The lady answered, "You can come to my place, park for the night and stay for my eclipse party." Ruth said "Okay." I came out and introduced myself and with that off we went to who knows where, following a lady named Karen.

If you don't know where you are going, a last name doesn't matter either.

Before speeding off Karen warned us "There is no cell phone connection once past the graveyard. I will slow down when we get there in case you need to use the phone, because once past it the signal goes dead, but I do have Wi-Fi at home."

It was a challenge following Karen, she must have thought my vehicle was an overgrown slot car the way she was driving, but the Go-Go Bus did good, only lagged behind a bit.

Here we were on some mountain road, following a speeding car. Ruth didn't worry but I was apprehensive as I didn't initiate the conversation to get a good feel for whoever this lady was. But God does work in mysterious ways and we were sure on a mysterious path alright.

We arrived to her house and no one was around except Karen and her barking dogs. She tried to convince me to drive down the dirt trail and park by the river, and in the morning we would wake to one beautiful site. She also asked if we had flashlights, and if we did to go ahead and explore her property. We didn't explore and I decided to stay under their street lamp, if you could call it that.

We were about to pull the curtains and call it a night when the husband came home, introductions were made, our doors were locked, and their dogs kept sentry duty with occasional barking through the night. Well, it will be interesting to see what morning brings. With that thought I shut off the lights.

It's amazing how different a place looks in the daytime. Karen's property was not spooky at all, but it sure was rural as can be. I was concerned where I parked. It was too close to the road, but found out that the road is a dead end with only two families living on it. Karen's family was one and the other we were warned "Don't go near them, they're rednecks and don't like strangers."

Karen didn't exaggerate when she said we would wake up to some beautiful scenery, it was an understatement. They have such a wonderful spread. Her parents bought the land in 1972 and built the house right next to Rocky River.

My thoughts then briefly went back to "Where is Janet?" The ranger said to stay away from Rock Island. Janet and her family could be enjoying all this. Oh well, they might be tied up in some traffic jam fighting for a spot to view the eclipse.

We offered our help with setting up for the eclipse party, but Karen already had everything under control. I decided to hurry to a store and buy something to contribute to it. The options were to drive back into McMinnville, or much closer was the HWY 30 Market, which is where we went. I walk in, Gary the owner says "Hey, neat vehicle." I introduce myself. He asks to see my book. From there it went like this: "Sure, we can do some swapping." So I ordered a fried pork chop sandwich, a ham and cheese sandwich, (both were delicious, especially the pork chop) a two liter Sun Drop pop, a water melon and a newspaper. Gary received the book.

It was now back to Karen and Michael's place, but not before stopping at the cemetery, the mountain top graveyard where the cell phone signal lives, but dies once you leave. I wanted to check on my phone messages, then we would return and await the big event, the eclipse. No messages! What happened to Janet?

When we returned they had everything set up right on the bank of the river. While waiting I enjoyed a quick dip. Wow, was that refreshing! Talk about cold mountain water!

Karen had more than enough food, but only two friends showed, plus Ruth and I. I stood back for a minute and pondered this: Here I am enjoying what possibly could be a once in a lifetime event with people I just met; now that's the way to make lasting memories.

Mountain Top Graveyard
Where the Cell Phone Signal Lives

So what were my thoughts on the great eclipse? I was late jumping on the bandwagon for joining in on the hype and excitement. When Janet mentioned going down to Tennessee to see the eclipse, I viewed it more as an opportunity to travel. But traveling down there, that was all people were talking about. The newspapers had headlines such as "Schools to close Monday for eclipse."

Quietly the excitement was building inside of me. Then standing there with people I just met who were really into it made me giddy, like a child on Christmas morning. The eclipse started right on time, about 1:30 p.m. Karen commented and laughed that Ruth and I drove all this way to see the eclipse, but weren't equipped with eclipse glasses, so back and forth we shared what they had.

Then slowly, very slowly, the moon started covering up the sun. When the eclipse was in full, what was a hot day of low 90's cooled down a good 20 degrees. Then it got quiet, very serene. An owl or something cooed or hooted, but that was the only sound, well besides us yelping and howling at the moon. I almost wish now I had shut up to enjoy it more. But what I thought would be darkness, like at midnight, was more twilight-like. I also thought it would last much longer, but as quickly as the sun was covered, it slowly was being uncovered. It was still fascinating to witness and something I won't forget. During the hoopla we tipped our glasses and saluted the event. What was that, firewater? Yowee! It sure heated me up in a hurry, quicker than the outside temperature rose.

After the eclipse it was kayaking time and floating down the river that runs through their property. I am not the best swimmer, so was reluctant, but after some prodding and coaxing by Michael I got into a kayak and I am sure glad I did. Besides, I sensed that Michael was truly disappointed when I balked, but was sincerely happy when I did. Both Michael and Karen really enjoy sharing their blessings of living where they do, and their generosity meant a lot to us. What wonderful people!

The water was as they said, not that deep, but cold, very cold. At the far end of their property on the river is a cave opening, and out of it flows a spring. The water flowing out was frigid, just amazing. After experiencing what I did, I told Michael I would make sure Ruth would try the kayak. He thanked me. That spoke volumes of his personality.

After Ruth navigated the river, hugs and handshakes were given with repeated "Thank you's" for opening their house to us. It was now time to hit the byways and highways for the long trek back home, but not before going in circles, literally. After realigning my bearings it was smooth sailing. Maybe on the way back home we would find Janet?

Suppertime hit while driving through Sparta, Tennessee. A little restaurant named Jack's Top BBQ looked inviting. Walking towards the front door a man asked what I was driving and where I was from. When I told him he exclaimed "You drove to Tennessee in that!" "Yes sir, I did." He was from North Carolina.

The buzz about the eclipse was still going on, even inside Jack's restaurant where they were handing out Moon Pies with every meal. I met a lady whose family was originally from Akron, Ohio and other people from North Carolina and Georgia.

The whole experience at Jack's was wonderful! We ordered their fish platter which was great. Also, the corn bread was delicious, the BBQ chicken was good, service excellent and the owner Jack was friendly and fun to kid with. Jack is a Christian patriot that serves a good meal. What more can you ask for?

My eye lids were heavy and I believe it was in the town of Cookeville that I decided to find a place to park for the night. Or was it Oak Ridge? Or was it somewhere else, but for sure it was in Tennessee? I was puttering along the main thoroughfare of whatever town I was in, looking for a spot when driving in the opposite direction a cop passed me. He turned around and got right on my tail. The first drive I found I took a sharp turn into it. The cop did the same. I got out asking where is a safe place to park and was greeted with "GET BACK IN YOUR VEHICLE!" Whoa! "Wait, I only want to..."GET BACK IN YOUR VEHICLE NOW!" He was hiding behind his car door and called for backup.

This is crazy! Earlier in the trip I was asked about the purse heist, now I am being treated like one of the most wanted. Finally when backup arrived the usual list of questions followed. After running my license the policeman came back and then asked "What's going on?" I hand him a postcard and proceed to tell him, I was only trying to inquire about where to park. "Oh, I am sorry. When I saw you driving so slow and then making an abrupt turn with you getting out I didn't know what was going on." I was finally directed to where I could shut my rolling home down for the night and that was that.

Morning was beautiful! OK, for those who know me let me clarify this, otherwise they will say that's a lie, Carey doesn't do mornings. Well then, noon was beautiful, but it was still morning to me. The route home had us passing close to Cumberland Falls, Kentucky, the Niagara Falls of the South as some call it. Of course a quick stop to see that, I always take the time to view it when nearby. I never tire of seeing it.

You know, looking at this story, I am sure some minister out there can come up with a sermon. It would include first the flood, then the moon blotting out the sun, and now the fall. Anyway....

Ruth wanted KFC. Yes, KFC. Why, when we have it in Ohio? Well, we were in Kentucky, the birthplace of KFC, so why not. The original restaurant was in Corbin, Kentucky. (Just some trivia for you.) After eating and licking our fingers we drove straight home and concluded the trip.

Oh, what about Janet? We never did find Janet! Kind of like, "Where's Waldo?" Well, we never saw him either!

Chapter Six

Directions to Where I Live

I meet the most interesting people when I travel. Below you will find directions copied as I received them from a friend who wanted me to visit.

"Are you coming to visit?" "Yes, if I ever figure out these directions I will."

"Before get to Arby's restaurant on Main Street in Morse, Kentucky. The First Federal Savings and Loan Bank is next to Arby's restaurant. Turn onto Hargis Avenue from Main Street by First Federal Savings and Loan Bank building. Turn right off Main Street to Hargis Avenue. Arby's restaurant and bank building is on right side going up Main Street. When turn on Hargis Avenue behind bank building there is red brick house. After past red brick house on right. Turn right and will be on Sun Street. When turn on Sun Street there is yellow house. After past yellow house there is two-story white house. The two-story white house is where my apartment is. The white house will have number 1228 on it. I live in apartment three. My name will be on mailbox for apartment three in small letters."

"OR Buddy turn in Arby's restaurant and it will bring (the road) to my apartment."

Just in case you did figure out the directions, the name of the town was changed. I don't think my friend would want people coming over and saying "Hello! I found the directions to your place in the book *Cruising Across America!*"

Chapter Seven

To Hell and Back

Well, I am back from Hell, and what a trip it has been! With me, even the most mundane things like going up to Detroit to fix my engine brings excitement.

Let's start from the beginning

I picked up Jeff, who was eagerly waiting with his bags and toolset. He said "I thought you might need the tools." Thinking to myself, why, Ter's got a garage full? But not wanting to be rude, I told Jeff it was a good idea. Later on that tool set turned out to be a very important.

We made it a little more than a mile from my house when a lady ran a stop light and almost smashed into the side of the Go-Go Bus. What an eye opener that was. After avoiding that near collision it was onto the freeway.

Trying to make up lost time to be at Ter's by 5:00 p.m., I had the bus humming along at close to 70, which is quite fast for this vehicle. But I figured if something did happen to the engine, would it really matter because I was going up there to fix the bus anyway?

About 65 miles from Cleveland the bus started hissing and smoking, and the temperature gauge read "Inferno." I quickly pulled over and right before shutting it off the engine coughed, wheezed, and went BANG! I thought for sure my high speed driving done did it. I peaked inside the doghouse and coolant was everywhere. Hanging inside out was my fan belt. For sure the engine had to be seized. Ter' has a big heart! If I was in Toledo, I'm positive he would come to the rescue, but Sandusky?

What can you do at a time like this? That's exactly what I thought also. I opened all the windows and took a berm side nap. Twenty-eight minutes later I stirred from my sleep, took Jeff's tool box (I told you Jeff to bring the tools!) and put the fan belt back on. Now came the really hard decision of using the water to fill the radiator or saving it for coffee. It was my engine and us driving, but on the other hand I was sacrificing a pot of coffee. I finally decided on filling the rad.

Turned the key and it sounded OK. Why that happened is beyond me. I told Jeff to put the radio away. I wanted to keep my ears open for any other sound that may pop up. It was sad to, Rush was on a roll with all new facts on – OK I won't start.

Rambling down the road quite a bit slower, nothing eventful happened for the next 75 miles. Gosh, no excitement for 75 miles; what a boring life I lead. Then suddenly like a misaimed Iraqi scud missile, a long white object nailed the front of the bus. KABAAAM! It appeared to come from the Jeep with a bike carrier that was in front of me. This happened a short distance from an exit. The jeep exited and seemed to speed up while doing this. I immediately thought he was trying to get away. The chase was on. The scud missile carrier black Jeep is pulling away with traffic behind, but look, it's the two-tone purple rolling "love hut" making its move. I caught him at a red light and yelled "Hey, did something fly off your car?" "No, I didn't see anything." Light changes and he quickly takes off and makes a quick right. The Go-Go Bus in hot pursuit stays right on his bumper. Finally a stop sign! I jump out and yell "WAIT!" Cringing at what I might find, I slowly turned around to survey the damage. Whatever hit it left the big E in DODGE hanging and smashed my license plate frame. Minimal damage was done, so after a brief exchange of words I said "Forget it" and took off.

OK, finally at Ter's and.... Drum roll please – its TADAHHHH: 5:15 p.m., only 15 minutes past my expected arrival. Ter' greets me with a hug, confetti streams down and marching girls appear. I knew I could do it.

Not wanting to waste time, Ter' prods me to "let's get with it." We change into our surgical garb and start extracting parts from the sickly Go-Go Bus. Ter' put his ear to the engine then looks me in the eye and tells the bad news "It's a wrist pin." No, no, please tell me it ain't so! Ter' says "We'll tear it apart further in the morning and I can pinpoint exactly what cylinder." We button it up for the night.

About 9:00 a.m. while still sleeping in the bus I feel it being jacked up. Chasing the cobwebs from my head I thought maybe I was in East Cleveland and they were jacking up my vehicle to steal the tires. I open the door and there is Ter' with a big grin and oozing confidence. "Ready to get the van running?" It was as if in the middle of the night the Mopar god came to him in a vision and said "YOU will fix the bus!" Ter' seemed so assured that I forgot I didn't have my coffee yet and began helping him.

He dropped the oil pan and quickly found the ailment. It wasn't the wrist pins but bearings. Now the real fun begins. Where do you find parts for a slant on a Saturday? Why any parts store; it can't be that bad. Wrong! Three and a half hours of driving around in large circles searching for bearings turned into a scenic, narrated tour given by Ter'. We hit the inner city, the outer city, the posh suburbs, every imaginable parts store in a 70-mile radius of Motown. No bearings!

Then suddenly it seemed as if I was in the Twilight Zone! We went to this house/machine shop that was off the main road about 500 feet or so with a gate and hidden by trees. Somehow we left the city and ended up in the country. There were these men, all with long Amish beards and wearing overalls, a woman was pushing a baby stroller around the barn machine shop and the clincher – a fenced pen with an honest to goodness coon dog. That's right, we were in Kentucky, or so it appeared. Unfortunately, after scrounging around, no bearings turned up, so it was back to the bustles of Detroit.

During all this driving Ter' was on the phone either making calls or receiving them. His phone was ringing more than the local pizza joint on a Friday night. Each call ended with "Thanks, we will try that parts store." I was ready to give up and told him "We tried!" Ter' turned and gave me this icy stare and said "You don't understand, this has turned into a quest, kinda like the Holy Grail, we don't give up!" Another call comes in. I say "Please God, let this be good news." SHAZAAM! It was! A friend up north called with news that Mazza Auto Parts has the bearings.

We speed off to Waterford, run into the place because they were keeping it opened just for us, and standing at the counter was a guy named Joe holding the box of bearings up high. "Is this what you're looking for?" He blows on the box and the dust goes flying. Absolutely! I pay and we excitedly speed back to fix the Go-Go Bus.

Ter' wanted to go cruising before the night ended. Was it possible, can we, could we fix the bus in time? Yeppers, we sure did! The way Ter' worked was as if he was in a pit crew at the NASCAR track. Not only were the bearings remedied, but also a bunch of other little ailments as well. Boy, does the slant sound sweet, like a baby V8.

We clean up and jump into Ter's '66 Plymouth Signet drop top. He decides to go to Doogans on Woodward Ave. Am I dreaming? Cruising the famous strip in a convertible. Life is good. All the way there he brags about Doogans burgers: "You gotta try one!" We sit upstairs, he orders the Big Chief burger and I order the pasta and shrimp. HUH? I couldn't help it. I weakened while looking at the menu. I am sure the burgers were as Ter' advertised – delicious!

Now off to cruise the strip. I started waving at people. Ter' says "Don't do that." I responded by saying "Picked that up in Kentucky, people wave at everyone down there." Ter' spoke up and said "Not here you don't. In the Bluegrass State people hoot n holler, in the Motor City you cruise and look cool like a well-rehearsed movie." At one section we cruised through there were bars, clubs, and a theater playing a Michael Moore movie. I wanted to stand up and give the Gettysburg Address. It was quickly frowned upon so I sat back once again and looked cool.

We ended the night at Ter's place discussing politics, A100's and our favorite movies with chase scenes. We came up with this list: Bullet, French Connection, The Seven-Ups, and Brewster McCloud. We were invited to stay, but after all Ter' did I couldn't impose on him any longer. Jeff and I started our journey home about 2:00 a.m.

Not having to be back until late Sunday, I asked Jeff "Do you really want to head back, let's find a campground." What a joke this turned out to be. Once you get outside the Detroit area it is sprinkled with little towns. Most seem as if they have been forgotten. We grabbed the map and Jeff chose Seven Lakes State Park. Jeff is very good with directions, but we couldn't figure out why we weren't agreeing on the route to take. Eventually we ended up at Holly State Recreation Area about 5:00 a.m. That's when I realized I was looking at the wrong park on the map. Oh well!

Not wanting to pay for a campsite for a few hours, we drove to the beach area which was closed due to bad roads. Oh boy! It was now sunrise; we had to park soon or no sleep. We drove around the park looking for any spot to pull over. No luck, so we left. Eventually we found a doctors' parking lot to sleep in.

Woke up about noon when a patrol car pulled in and had his drug-sniffing dog circle the Go-Go Bus. That's not the first time this has happened. Hmmm, don't know why! The patrolman knocked on the door and said "ID's please." Then the list came next. "Do you have any drugs, knives, weapons, guns, AK47's!" As quickly as he rattled off the list I kept up with the "No's" until he asked for a "BINGO DABBER?" I thought I must be getting old. Is it a new weapon or is it a drug? I asked "What's a bingo dabber?" He looked at me funnier than when he first saw the bus. "You know, a bingo dabber, a bingo dotter, something you mark bingo cards with." He must have been following me for a while and kept track of all the purchases I made at garage sales; he's an IRS agent in disguise. Nothing was found, but he made us check out of the doctors' lot.

We drove around, still looking for a lake or beach, but all of them in Michigan charge. Yes, even if you want to enter only to eat a lunch you pay $8, but at the county parks you pay $5.

We gave up not wanting to pay a fee and I said "Let's eat at the cemetery, its quiet, peaceful and free!" So that's what we did. After eating lunch we looked at the map to head home, but took one final detour since we were this far – a drive through Hell, Michigan, at least to snap a picture of the town sign.

Hell is a very small place with the post office in a food mart. The local attraction is the Halloween/ice cream store called Screams with a Crematory inside. Pretty neat! The town drunk, Dave, happened to be hanging around, so of course I had to chat. Dave was like the unofficial/official welcoming committee for Hell. He told me to park and make supper there in the lot, because by this time it was almost 7:00 p.m. I made tacos and offered him one. Dave said "No thanks" and we should have eaten at the Dam Inn which has excellent food. Hell is situated by a small lake.

After feasting on tacos I decided to play with the town drunk. I would occasionally squeeze my whoopee cushion and make grunts while apologizing. While laughing and saying "OH MY" repeatedly, Dave told Jeff he should find another way home. He never caught on to what I was doing.

We prepared the Go-Go Bus for takeoff and headed back home to Clevo. What a fun and eventful weekend it was!

So I wrote this whole story for just one statement, just one and that one statement is this: I think you should go to Hell and eat at the Dam Inn.

42

Chapter Eight

The Shower

Have you ever wanted to take a long, hot, quiet, relaxing shower? I was staying at a campground in southern Ohio. At this campground the men's shower room was set up with shower stalls lined up one after another. Each stall had a curtain and small changing area before the shower.

As I entered I heard two giggling boys in shower stalls next to each other. As I proceeded to shower, their talking and laughter got louder and louder, so I decided to have some fun.

I blew a raspberry on my wet arm. This momentarily got their attention, but they went right back to noisily giggling and talking. I did it again, but this time with a little groan. One boy said, "Did you hear that?" It didn't silence them for long, they continued making noise. So, once more I did it, but louder and with more relieving moans.

This really caught the boys' attention and they both hushed up. Now I was the one having fun, so I blew a much longer raspberry with a loud "OHHHH." Almost at the same time they nervously said to each other, "Oh my gosh! Let's hurry up and get out of here!" Suddenly it got even quieter, the water stopped, and one said "Ready? Let's go!" and they both ran out.

Poor boys, but I got my quiet, relaxing shower!

Chapter Nine

Christmas Events Ohio-Style

Here are reviews of three annual Christmas events in Ohio; no twists, just straight, honest reviews. The first is Berlin's Nativity Parade, the second is Cleveland's Winterfest and the third is the Christmas Parade in Jefferson. Berlin's event had nothing to do with Santa Claus, Cleveland's had nothing to do with Christmas and Jefferson had little to do with Christ's birth, so all bases were covered: religious, politically correct, and secular.

Nativity Parade in Berlin, Ohio

Berlin is a small town in the middle of Ohio Amish country. Their Christmas event is a nativity parade, and it has nothing to do with Santa or any make-believe Christmas fantasy. It is all about the real reason for the season, which is celebrating Christ's birth. It is held annually the first Friday after Thanksgiving. I found this event to be uplifting with a very homey traditional feel of days gone by. People arrive early to browse the shops and to grab a spot on the parade route; both sides of the street get filled with onlookers. Local churches set up tables offering free hot chocolate and cookies.

The procession of trumpeters, live animals – including camels and shepherds with sheep – and marchers dressed in period clothes for the time of Christ, was refreshingly different. After the

44

last group of trumpeters passed, that signaled the end of the parade. People immediately got in line and followed behind for a candle lighting ceremony at the square. The square had a small stage with a singer leading the crowd in Christmas carols. It was a solemn occasion, and the light snow showers the night we attended added a special touch for a memorable evening.

Winterfest in Cleveland, Ohio

The next event, "Winterfest," was held on Public Square in Cleveland, Ohio. Of the three events I attended, this was my least favorite. It had nothing to do with Christmas! I think I may have heard Christmas mentioned once on the stage occupied by various entertainers.

I also never saw a Santa Claus. If there was one, I didn't see him. Even the name Winterfest is ridiculous because winter doesn't start until December 21st and this was held soon after Thanksgiving. Winterfest makes me think of sledding, skating, and snow, but not Christmas, and maybe that's the way they want it. The fireworks ending the night were good though.

Christmas Parade in Jefferson, Ohio

The third ceremony was Jefferson's Christmas Parade, which had Santa present, but had little to do with Jesus' birth even though the M.C. started it off with a statement for love of God and country, and local churches do have floats in the parade. I also liked this event. Only in small-town America can you find tow trucks, snow plows and semis decorated with lights and trimmings. Besides trucks and fire trucks from nearby towns, they had the Blue Belles from the local senior center, Boy Scouts, Girl Scouts, and numerous other groups like the Snowmobile Club. It was festive and fun, and most importantly it was what a small town event should be – family oriented! The parade lasted about 30 minutes, and is held annually the first Saturday in December.

Also held on the same day of the Jefferson's Christmas Parade is the Old-Fashioned Williamsburg Christmas Celebration at the historic 19th Century Jefferson Depot Village.

The Depot Village has among other events a candlelight walk and a live nativity in the church barn built in 1849. Many of the buildings, including the depot, are open to the public for a casual walk through.

The Victorian House even has a butler waiting to greet you and warm wassel with a tray of cookies to sample.

Merry Christmas!

Note: The historic 19th Century Jefferson Depot Village is a fun place to visit also during the summer, not just at Christmas. They have costumed tour guides to take you around. You can even make reservations for groups, weddings, reunions, parties, and meetings.

Chapter Ten

A Christmas Memory

Since I just wrote about Christmas, I thought I would add one more holiday story that goes back to about the early 90's. It was Christmas Eve and I was returning home after visiting Emerson in Hillsboro and Carl and Judy Rudd of Blue Creek, both towns in southern Ohio. I was in no hurry as there was no reason to rush home. The family was celebrating Christmas Day, but not Eve.

I was hungry but nothing was open. Back then it was mostly independent restaurants that closed during the holidays and the corporations didn't start with the late night hours regardless of the season. Finally after about an hour plus on the road I found a restaurant. I don't remember exactly where, but I believe it was somewhere south of Columbus.

It was just like in the movies, traveling on Christmas Eve through the snow with little to no traffic and spotting a sign that blinked open. The restaurant was like an oasis. I can still vision the place that harkened back to an earlier time. It was dimly lit, lots of wood, wooden floors, paneling, and chairs at tables with table cloths. The only ones in the restaurant were the waitress and the cook. Just picture perfect. But all of that is not why I remember this Christmas Eve restaurant memory. No, not at all! I remember it because the food was so bad – just terrible! What a memory!

Chapter Eleven

Anything Open?

We were outside of Orlando when the Go-Go Bus started to spit and knock. Someone told us that there was a 24-hour auto parts store open. We took directions and headed there. I found it weird that a parts store would be open 24/7 as I never heard of such a thing and thought maybe the guy was just fooling with us. But sure enough, when we arrived at 2:00 a.m. it was open. I was able to get what was needed to make the bus run right.

I went to install the part in the parking lot of the store when a homeless man and his girlfriend approached me. He offered to help. I said "I am on vacation, you want to put it on, go for it." The man knew exactly what he was doing. I gave him a few bucks, a sweater to his woman and some cookies for his effort. I am sure he was proud in front of his girl that he was able to do something to help their plight – and mine!

Before leaving I went back inside the store and asked if there was a place to eat nearby. The worker laughed and said there is NOTHING open around here – NOTHING!

I guess a 24-hour parts store doesn't count, and now I also know why the homeless guy was hanging out there.

Chapter Twelve

Fall Festival Summer Fun

One of the things I love doing during the summer months is attending festivals and fairs, especially in towns I've never been to before. Most festivals are pretty much the same anymore and not holding true to their title. Grape festivals have little to do with grapes, corn festivals – same thing, so going to unfamiliar towns adds some excitement. And really, a summer isn't a summer unless you go to at least one festival or fair no matter how lame.

I went to a website dedicated to Ohio Festivals. Listed was a Fall Festival being held in little Scio, Ohio, population under 800. The festival is held annually the third week of August. Scio is about 100 miles from Cleveland and is close to Leesville Lake and nature area. It is a quaint little town with a very short main street, a barbershop that looks as if it was remodeled the last time in the 50's, a bakery that also doubles as a cluttered second hand store (the peanut butter chocolate chip cookies were good), an abandoned train depot, the paved Conotton Creek Trail suitable for walking, biking or wheel chairs (I never did see the creek. The path is at least 20 feet from the creek and lined with bushes and trees) and a covered bridge. The place is a real throwback to yesterday. There still are pockets in America where little towns cling to the past and things change so much slower.

I attended the Fall Festival on Saturday, the last day. Because of a detour that put me miles off course I missed the children's parade which I believe was the big event. People were still sitting on benches and lining the sidewalk, just sitting and conversing in no big hurry to go. I was snapping photos of the town when a young man walked into the shot I just took. He turned around and apologized. I said "You are OK, I was aiming high at the wooden sign for the Scio Municipal Building. I find it fascinating." The sign was painted black and written in white lettering was Scio Municipal Building – Mayor's Office – Council Chambers – Clerks Office. He said "I see it every day and it's just an old sign, no big deal." I replied back, "Well, coming from the city it is homey and a throwback to simpler times. I love it." He in turn said "I guess you from the city get impressed by things in little towns, we in little towns get impressed with the big city." "You're right," I said.

We made formal introductions. His name was Keith. I said to him "Another thing that fascinates me even more than the sign is why is this festival called a Fall Festival when it is still summer? I'm puzzled." Keith had a simple explanation. He explained that the Fall Festival is over 80 years old and maybe back then when the festival started this was fall before global warming changed seasons.

Ah yes, a simple reason given in a simple town. I love it!

Chapter Thirteen

Cherry Springs State Park

This is a recount of my trip to Cherry Springs State Park, which is one of the darkest spots on the eastern seaboard. It is so dark astronomers come from all over to stargaze and take photos. Cherry Springs is located in Susquehannock State Forest in Potter County, Pennsylvania. Potter County is billed as God's Country because of its unspoiled beauty.

I love trips where nothing is planned but everything works out as though they were, and that's how this trip went. The only things planned were seeing the dark park and maybe the Coudersport Ice Mine, other than that we would wing it. Likewise with the routes, I only jotted down 90 East to 86 East to Olean, New York, then head south into Pennsylvania and once there ask for directions.

Unfortunately the weather didn't cooperate. I joked on the way that I hope the darkest spot on the eastern seaboard isn't made even darker by the cloud cover. My sad prediction came true as it was cloudy or rainy for two days of the three-day trip. At least the last day coming home was sunny and summer-like.

Our first official stop on the road was a restroom break on Rt. 86 in Chautauqua Lake. This rest area is one of the nicest and most extravagant I've ever seen. Way over the top! The view of

Chautauqua Lake is just awesome. You could actually spend an afternoon here picnicking; it's that nice.

After our break it was back onto Rt. 86 until a road construction detour had the freeway blocked and threw us off and onto Rt. 417 in Salamanca. This actually worked out for the better because Rt. 417 runs right into Olean.

We ate lunch outside of Olean in a little place that was set up more like a house with mismatched chairs and tables. The food was good. I asked our waitress for directions towards Coudersport, Pennsylvania. She tried drawing a map. After a few futile attempts she finally made one that was legible. The cook saw it and said "Forget all that, just stay on 417 until 44 and that will get you there." I felt bad for the waitress, so told her I would save her map and hang it on my fridge.

As I mentioned, I didn't make many plans for this trip but everything went as if I did. The cook's directions took us right into Coudersport. Once in town we immediately located a grocery store to buy food because we didn't bring any so we could travel light. In the store parking lot I asked a man parked next to me if he knew how to get to Cherry Springs. He did and gave us directions. Then at Cherry Springs there was an unexpected surprise; there was a sign that read Star Party – Public Night.

Since we didn't preregister for the star gazing event we couldn't set up camp with the astronomers and stargazers.

However, they did say we were welcome to join them for the event and some may even let us use their telescopes. They informed us about the rules which were also posted on signs: NO flashlights without a red filter; keep flashlights pointed down and NO LASERS of any kind.

The registration tent directed us across the road to a public campground. After driving around and back and forth trying to find a level spot (seems I do this ritual every time I'm at a campground), we finally agreed on one. And what happened? The campsite wasn't as level as it looked and the Go-Go Bus immediately got stuck in the wet grass. A few attempts were tried at getting out but the wheels kept digging in deeper as it was sliding back closer and closer to the trees. It didn't matter we were parked on a slant, we were staying put. A ranger happened to drive by and told us the park maintenance could tow us out in the morning. The only problem was we couldn't leave to buy firewood or see what was in the area.

Instead of just waiting in the Go-Go Bus for nightfall to arrive we walked back to the star party. I was proud of my 50-power binoculars I brought along until I saw what those people had; the size of their telescopes was amazing. One man had a cannon-like telescope with wires connected to a computer. He was showing the photos he took of different galaxies and formations. Everyone that saw them was wowed.

We excitedly went back to our campsite to cook supper and wait for dark and the star show to begin. The skies had other plans though. The rains came and came hard. It stopped raining close to the same time we finished dinner so we found our way back to the star party. The rains stopped but the clouds remained so many of the astronomers just gave up and went to bed. Others sat waiting and some went to the canteen that was set up that served drinks and snacks which was lit by red lights only. It was fun sitting there drinking coffee. The girls manning the counter gave us hope when they told us the weather service said it would clear a little after midnight. I asked one girl if she believed in global wetting. The look she gave said she was clueless.

We clock watched and had an hour to kill, so Paul suggested we find the man with the computer and ask to see his photos again. We found him and his friend and made formal introductions. Their names were Jonathan and Rex from White Plains, New York. They were beyond disgusted. They arrived five days earlier and it was either rain or cloud cover since. Jonathan was more than enthused to show us his photos once more.

All of us were briefly elated when a little past midnight the skies cleared just about on time. Jonathan started to get his gear together when it clouded right back up. So what do you do when you are damp and chilled under a cloudy sky in August? You complain about global warming and talk politics. After agreeing on just about everything, we left.

It was so peaceful but eerie walking back to the campsite; no one around, dark skies and small flashlights. I thought I heard what sounded like a waterfall so I told Ruth "Follow me; let's go investigate." Paul opted out and stayed put. We walked a good distance down this curvy mountain road getting closer and closer to the sound of water when I realized it wasn't a waterfall but the edge of a rain storm. I could literally see the dividing line between rain and no rain. I grabbed Ruth and started running as the rain was on our heels. The three of us made it back just in time before the heavens really opened up. We called it an early night.

Cherry Springs - Waterfall or Rain?

I had such a rough night of sleep, it was awful. I was so uncomfortable because of the slant the bus was parked on I kept rolling. Somehow I managed to stay in bed till 10:00 a.m.

We awoke to more rain but it didn't matter if it was, it was time to get the Go-Go Bus out. The day before, I found a snow fence thrown in the woods. I thought if I could put it in front of the wheels the bus might gain enough traction and drive out. So Paul and I went on a long hike to retrieve it. It was fruitless; all that work to drag the fence out of the woods in the rain was for nothing. The park crew still had to tow us out and they did it in no time.

Leaving there our first stop was for gas at a throwback of a place, Keener's Country Store. It's a gas station that has groceries, ice cream, souvenirs and gift shop all in one. They informed us the Coudersport Ice Mine, one of the places I wanted to see, was just a short drive.

Unfortunately, just my luck, the Coudersport Ice Mine, the eighth wonder of the world, something I wanted so see since a kid, had no ice because of an unusually wet summer. But another side of me was pleased, the cheap side. The owner, Gary Buchsen, gave tours anyway of the iceless ice mine free of charge. Even though there was very little ice, it was still bone chilling cold in there. Weird! The talk from Gary was so interesting and informative that even without the ice it was well worth it – even if it was free!

Because I made very little plans, which I do on a lot of my trips, I just ask whomever for sites to see or things to do. And that's what I did at the Coudersport Ice Mine, I asked the lady at the counter. She didn't disappoint and recommended a few places to see. On her list was the Lumber Museum in nearby Galeton, the other places were the Austin dam site, the Austin museum, and on top of that the Austin Dam Show music festival was going on. We chose to head to Austin. The brochure we were handed for the Dam Park states it has Wi-Fi but no cell phone usage. I just found that interesting.

I came up with the plan before going to Austin to go back to the grocery store in Coudersport, buy food for lunch and cook it in Austin. We came out of the store and a guy approached me and said "Nice vehicle. We left you a drink token for the Hotel Critteden on your windshield." He then asked if we were there for the '69 reunion. I was taken aback, thinking, "Do I look that old that I could have graduated in 1969?" He also asked "Are you going to the Dam Show?"

We drove towards Austin and started to pull in the Austin Dam Memorial Park thinking it was the site of the museum. An attendant stopped us and asked "Are you one of the bands for the Dam Show?" He directed us towards town.

The Austin Historical Museum was terrific and free. Not much is left of Austin since the great flood caused by the dam break way back in 1911 and the closing of the paper mill in 1944. What is left is like a time warp. As we were leaving the museum a man pulled up in a truck and asked "Did you get to see the museum?" We told him we did and were just leaving. He replied "Well, if you didn't I was going to open it up for you." Small town manners, love it!

Right outside of town was a roadside pull off with one weathered picnic table and a historical sign describing the closure of the Bayless Paper Mill whose remains were directly across the river; a perfect place for a quick lunch of freshly made tacos.

After lunch I briefly stopped on the road overlooking the Dam Show and took a few photos. We then went back to Coudersport and again back to the same grocery store to shop for our dinner before heading to a campsite for the night. In the parking lot a young man came up to me and said "WOW, what a cool vehicle HEY, the Dam Show is happening, you should go, you would fit in." We came out of the store and a lady approached me and said "We saw you parked on the road above the Dam Show. We thought you were one of the bands. Are you? You should join us."

I asked Paul if we should get the free drink at the Hotel Crittenden or hit the road. He was all in favor of getting the drink so that was what we did.

The bartender at Crittenden gladly accepted our drink token and even served us hors d'oeuvres of shrimp, stuffed mushrooms and stuffed clams. Gourmet! The general manager, Chandra, came out to greet us in such a warm and friendly manner. She thought we were part of the '69 reunion, that's why the free drink token. It really threw them for a loop because the school colors are white and purple, close to the colors of the Go-Go Bus, and it's the same year of the reunion. Chandra didn't think we were from the class of '69, but that they hired us. She then said "The Dam Show is going on, you should go, it's a great time." Each time the Dam Show was mentioned and explained I acted surprised and said "Really!"

Chandra gave us a brief rundown on the Hotel Crittenden and some of its history. The hotel is where Eliot Ness wrote *The Untouchables*. Being from the Cleveland area I found that fascinating.

We left there and were in need of a map to find our way to a campground for the night. No problem, there was a Chamber of Commerce and artisan shop open past seven on a Saturday – how 'bout that! The man working gave me directions to a campground about five miles out of town on Rt. 6 along with plenty of brochures and maps. It seemed like on this trip every time we asked for directions it was always five miles this or that way.

We drove further than five miles but never found the campground so we pulled into a bar parking lot and asked someone who was also just pulling in. He said "Follow me, I will show you where to turn for a campground."

The name of the campground he directed us to was Sizerville State Park on Rt. 155, and not the one the Chamber of Commerce gave us directions to. It is a preregister campground which to me is a scam. You have to call a third party who registers you for a fee on top of the regular charge for the campsite. I wasn't about to call at 1:00 a.m. and possibly go through a host of prompts or them even saying we need advance notice – sorry! There was an empty site so we stayed.

I was glad we only parked for the night. I didn't like the campground. It was way to clean and sterile, meaning sites were manicured with very few trees; it just didn't have the feel of the great outdoors. We didn't pay at night, but in the morning Paul found the slot to deposit the money. I insisted, instead of leaving the money there, just let's drive to the camp office and pay. This turned out to be a blessing because we wanted to find a church and we did without having to leave the campground.

As we neared the park office we heard singing and music that got louder and louder; it was worship music. I told Paul and Ruth, "Well, we found a church!" It was a church picnic hosted by Port Allegany Alliance Church. The Pastor Joseph Beckley and the whole congregation greeted us with open arms. Ruth was happy because it was an Alliance church like the one she attended in the Philippines, and the pastor was happy that strangers had joined them. They invited us to stay for lunch, which we accepted. And after lunch we stayed to watch their ice bucket challenge. Upon leaving the pastor and many from the congregation thanked us again for joining them.

It was now time to find our way home, but of course the slow way home which was through Salamanca and the Alleghanys. The Indian museum in Salamanca was a bit of a disappointment. I thought being in Indian country it would be far better than any city museum. I really thought it lacked. A large part of it was dedicated to Lacrosse, which is no big deal to me, but according to the museum, Indians excel at it. What didn't disappoint though was driving through the Alleghanys. At first I was upset because they have toll booths that charge an entrance fee, but when we approached the person manning it waved us through. The scenery and beauty of the park was even a bigger blessing. We entered at the Salamanca entrance and exited at Quaker Lake.

Our drive home continued through Jamestown, New York. We found a place called Alfie's Restaurant, Home of Smuggler's Cove, and stopped there for supper. The fish fry labeled as Alfie's Famous Fish Fry lived up to its billing. I'm not sure how famous it is but it was real good. Besides the good meal I liked the décor of the place. It has such a retro old school look but the place isn't that old. Our waitress asked where we were coming from. We told her Quaker Lake in the Alleghanys. She replied "I know all about Quaker Lake. When they flooded that area to create the lake the school my dad went to is on the bottom." Her story reminded me of my grades in school which were all below C level, but that's another story!

From Jamestown we jumped on the freeway and headed home. Another memorable trip for sure.

Chapter Fourteen

Turf and Surf or Soup?

Fresh Air Pun

A group of friends and I were touring the back roads of Amish Country in Holmes County, Ohio.

The scenery was beautiful and the air was fresh. It was fresh until we approached a huge dairy farm with countless cows in a nearby pasture. The air changed quickly and was now unbearable. There is nothing like the odor of cow manure baking in the hot sun. It stunk badly.

I said without thinking "Aw yes, you can smell the dairy air now!"

Turtle Soup

I had turtle soup only once. It was at a restaurant called Crossroads Dinor in Edenborough, Pennsylvania.

The turtle soup was delicious, but it sure was slow getting to the table.

Chapter Fifteen

Letchworth and
Our Heaven-Sent Angels

I learned a very valuable lesson on this trip: Read the pamphlets they hand you at the camp office when you first arrive. Don't do as we did and read them after our night hike of exploring and our daytime hiking experience – and it was an experience! Reading the camp information first would have saved us from my attempt to walk us off into oblivion in the dark, and also would have shaved miles and hours off our daytime march.

It all started with me saying "Hey, I don't want to do the tourist thing and drive right up to the falls, let's hike!" The maps we had weren't marked the clearest as far as distance to certain points are concerned. However, this I do know, if we would have walked from the campground as I initially wanted to, it would have been about a 15-mile hike. But before that hiking marathon even started, the first night there we took a night hike and I was insistent on finding the river. Thank God we didn't find the river! The river's edge was at the bottom of a 600-foot steep cliff. Gee, I didn't know! Again we should have read the pamphlet first which states clearly "Steep Banks!" Hmmm, wonder if that's why the campground is named Highbanks?

But I'm getting way too far ahead. Let's rewind to the beginning.

It was one of those trips where everything went perfect. Even being able to get a campsite during peak leaf viewing time and a large event taking place was a miracle. When I called for a reservation the lady initially laughed but she checked anyway. Suddenly someone cancelled their reservation as we were speaking, so I grabbed it!

Our day of takeoff was just beautiful as was the whole weekend. You couldn't have asked for better fall weather: sunny, bright, warm days, a bit chilly with clear skies at night. Absolutely wonderful! Just everything, I mean everything, went perfect. I managed to be on time to register at the campground. I even found a farm stand that had corn. No big deal for anybody else, but to me it was.

I had such a taste for corn on the cob. I mean what's a campfire without corn to roast? Both stores we went to didn't have any, and then I realized corn was already out of season. So what a blessing it was to see just a short distance from our destination an old wooden, unmanned vegetable/fruit stand that still had ears of corn. It looked like a mirage. I spun the bus around, jumped out, deposited the cash in the tin can and grabbed six healthy ears. Isn't it amazing that in parts people still use the honor system. In Cleveland, not only the cash jar would be taken but also all the vegetables and the stand. It turned out that my excitement about finding corn was only shared by me. I found this out at our campsite when I roasted corn for everyone, but no one ate any.

After the excitement of finding corn, and Lisa still not sure where we were heading, we finally arrived at......Tadah, the entrance to the Highbanks campground in beautiful Letchworth State Park. It was quite busy at the camp office because of their big annual arts and crafts show taking place.

All the way there I worried if we may have a problem signing in to our campsite because I forgot the confirmation letter. They only reminded me twice on the phone and once by email: DO NOT FORGET YOUR CONFIRMATION LETTER OR......OK, OK, I won't forget it, but guess what? I still did. And wouldn't you know it, as we pull in two greeters, a lady and a man, greeted us with "Make sure you have your registration number when you sign in!" "OH BOY, uh ma'am I don't have it." "You don't have it." "No I left it at home on my desk." "You left your registration number at home. How did you get here with no license plate?" "OHHHH, that registration number, I thought you meant for our campsite." Both of them laughed.

Hey, to me a registration is the paper that comes with the license plate, a license plate is a license plate – not a registration number. When you are worrying about the campground registration number because they said you cannot sign in without it.....oh, never mind! Anyways, they never asked for the campground registration number so all that worrying was for nothing.

We check in, I unload, I set up the tent, I start the fire, I get the lantern going. I plug in my four-watt cassette radio which got us yelled at by an angry sleeping camper for being too loud, and I cook. But Lisa and Dave did help also, just trying to remember how. Dishes, that's right, they helped clean the dishes.

After our fireside dinner and a long night hike of trying to find the river's edge, which was just a warm up of things to come, we nestled into our cozy accommodations. Saturday morning God blessed us with picture perfect weather, temps about 70 degrees and sunny. Just a gorgeous fall day with vibrant colors! A quick breakfast of perked coffee and buttered toast in a frying pan ......mmm is that good; the only real way to eat toast! We straightened out the bus and campsite, threw our lunches and drinks into a Go-Go Handy Pack bag, then headed out for a three-hour hike, three-hour hike at the most, that is, and that would include back and forth.

The time we left our campsite and got on Park Road to head to the trails and falls was about 11:30 a.m. I drove to several overlook, picnic, and parking areas trying to figure out if we were close enough to start our hike. My goal was to start far away enough to take a nice afternoon hike, enjoy the trails, scenery, and see the falls, then get back to the campsite before dark to make plans for the evening. Our first stop was Gardeau Overlook. Nope! Too far! We can't even see a hint of the falls. On to St. Helena Picnic Area and we found the same thing. Then we went onto Eddy's and finally Tea Table where we met Mr. Photographer. Mr. Photographer, the man who told us "Oh, it's only a 30-minute hike to the falls from here, you can do it."

How we met Mr. Photographer was I pulled into another scenic overlook parking lot, and instead of getting out surveying the distance and wasting more time, I called him over and asked "How far to the falls?" I have to repeat what he said: "Oh, it's only a 30-minute hike to the falls from here, you can do it." We grabbed our bags, which weren't well equipped for our unplanned ordeal, and headed toward the path he pointed out. Just a short distance later there he was, Mr. Photographer.

Mr. Photographer had his camera set up on the edge of an overlook. I should have pushed him off right there; well at least his camera or maybe both. I asked him a few more questions like "Are you sure it's not far?" "No big deal, I did this hike many times." But then he continued on with a story of how he got stranded one winter day. Unfortunately no one picked up on this, not Dave, Lisa or me. He told us he brought along a sled to hold his camera equipment as he hiked to the falls that winter day. Now when I think of this, why a sled for only a 30-minute hike that was no big deal? On the way there the path was snow covered. On the way back the snow had melted from the sun. That's hint number two that this was not a 30-minute hike to the falls. To make a long story short.....nightfall was upon him, it was cold, but because the snow had melted off the trail, the sled wouldn't glide and he had to lug everything back. He even tried shouting to a helicopter flying low overhead. Hint number three we also missed: He was praying for the helicopter to land and rescue him for only a 30-minute hike back, and he was already more than halfway into the hike? We said "Goodbye, thanks for the directions."

After four hours of hiking I started looking for that man. Thirty-minute hike! Thirty-minute hike! Four hours and still NO FALLS! FORGET THE FALLS! WHERE IS THAT MAN? I am sure you're asking yourself why we didn't turn back after four hours. Because around every bend and every clearing and every 100th tree we thought this is it, the falls can't be that much further, that man said it would only be 30 minutes and we're approaching four hours of hiking, so it just can't be that much further. That, and also we got to the point where, as Lisa said, "No way are we turning back. WE ARE ON A QUEST NOW."

And then I spotted a sign, a Glen Iris Inn sign. This put the spring back in my step as I was literally jumping for joy that the falls, which are by the inn, were surely just a few more marching steps ahead! My elation though was for naught as that sign was poorly marked. Thirty more minutes passed, it hit four o'clock and still no falls or inn in sight. But wait, what's that, a swimming pool? No past that! It's the Lower Falls Restaurant. Wahooooo! I said "Let's hurry up and make it to the falls so we can take a break and eat our lunches there." Lisa and I had our lunch that I prepared for the three of us the day before, but Dave ate his way before we even picked up Lisa in Erie, so he watched us eat.

We walked a short distance to the lower falls, I kicked off my shoes, we ate our lunch, rested for a bit, three minutes.....hmmm maybe four, and then we trod on to the upper falls. Time passes: 4:45 p.m., 5:00 p.m., 5:30 p.m., and Dave says "THATS IT, I AM DONE, YOU GUYS GO ON WITHOUT ME." Dave succumbed and was out. I tried perking him up, but no use. "LEAVE! I AM

69

TAKING FIVE MINUTES! GO! LEAVE ME ALONE!" Ouch! Lisa and I moved on with me questioning how will we find him or maybe he will hitchhike back; it's not good to get separated. I was concerned. Lisa could care less; she was still focused on the quest. But further down the trail to the middle falls, like a gust of wind out of nowhere, Dave reappeared with renewed spirits and enthusiasm and rejoined us.

Finally, drum roll.......the middle falls were in view! We made it, time about 6:00 p.m. Not bad, we started this trek close to 11:30 a.m. and it was supposed to be only a 30-minute hike, if that. But we didn't relish in the glory too long as the middle falls were only part of our goal, we still had a moderate distance to the upper falls. It was kind of sad actually because we were so worn out that the enthusiasm and awe of seeing the falls was wasted. Oh, I am sure Dave and Lisa enjoyed it but not nearly as much as if they were rested, plus not much time was spent enjoying the middle falls because our goal of seeing the upper falls still lied ahead.

At last we were approaching the upper falls, but I didn't let on that the final crescendo wasn't seeing them but climbing the railroad bridge above the falls. It is a must. So we get to the upper falls and Dave and Lisa are about to sit, relax and take it all in when I spring on them, "Come on, let's go." I am sure by now Lisa had thought I lost it or maybe in another life I was a deranged drill sergeant, but after some prodding and coaxing I talked them into climbing the railroad bridge that is clearly marked STAY OFF. NO TRESPASSING. Dave got to the base of the bridge, looked up and said "No way, you're nuts, have fun, goodbye." Lisa, being a good sport, or to shut me up, walked the steep incline to the bridge. What a site, breathtaking and YES, scary! If a train barrels through you either hold on or you jump off, it's not that wide of a bridge.

Atop Letchworth State Park's Trestle Bridge

The bridge is 820 feet long, 240 feet tall and almost directly above the upper falls that are over 70 feet tall. The deck of the bridge is steel grating that you can look through, which makes it even more nerve wracking walking on it. The railing on the sides are not really made for safety, just enough to keep someone from falling off. The bridge definitely wasn't made for pedestrian traffic, but who pays attention to details; we didn't and neither did a family who also was atop the bridge. Lisa and I were gingerly walking along holding the railing for dear life and here was this family taking a walk like it was nothing. They had a small child and no one was holding on to him. Their dog a few times started to slip through the tracks so they yanked him up by the leash. It was freaky watching the family and made us beyond nervous. So a couple of glances below to take in the breath-taking sight and a few at the family, then it was time to get out of there and face the grueling hike back.

So what about our heaven-sent angels as the title of this story suggests? Well, we had to walk back. If it took us about 7½ hours to walk to the falls and the time was now nearing 7:30 p.m.; that would mean we would not return to our campsite till about 2:00 a.m. or much later because of how tired we were. Just thinking about it was more painful than the pain in our feet! I tried to ask a few people in the parking lot for a ride, but got nowhere quick. Reluctantly we had to start walking, and as we were I put my thumb out to hitchhike, but no luck. I said to Lisa "Please, you try!" She did. Instantly a car pulled over. It was Bob and Linda, an elderly couple. They drove us all the way back to where the Go-Go Bus was parked and that's how they became our heaven-sent angels. Otherwise, who knows, we may still be wandering.

Letchworth State Park is located in upstate New York in Wyoming County. It is called the Grand Canyon of the East. I highly recommend a visit to the park. And make sure you read the park brochure before hiking, I recommend that also. And whatever you do, if you need directions do not ask a photo-grapher, it could be the one that lied and led us on a 7½ hour hike.

Chapter Sixteen

Night and Day

Walt is a pleasure to travel with. I always enjoy going on trips with him. He will just about see or do anything. Though, there is one thing that does interfere and can fray our nerves when we travel together. That one thing is our sleeping schedule. I am a night person and sleep in late even when traveling. Walt is more of a morning person, waking very early at home, on the road, and whether he has to work or not.

On one trip to southern Ohio and Kentucky with Walt I was doing everything I could to stay up later than normal so he would sleep in late and not wake me in the early AM hours. No matter how late I kept him up, he still woke up early.

Finally I blurted out "What's wrong with you? I have been doing everything I could to keep you up late so you would sleep in and you still wake early."

Walt replied "Well, what's wrong with you? I have been doing everything I could to wake you up early so you would sleep early and you still stay up late."

Sometimes you just can't win!

Chapter Seventeen

Mansfield Reformatory Trip

Before Take Off

On September 5th my sister Cindi, Jeff and I will be in Mansfield, Ohio touring the Mansfield Reformatory. We will be given a rules and regulations speech, followed by a 1½ hour guided tour. The best part of the tour is after the orientation the lights will be turned off, we will then be locked in the prison and on our own until 5:00 a.m. We're allowed to bring any device we want, tape and video recorders and/or ghost hunting apparatuses of any kind.

Besides the historical significance and the obvious spookiness of being in an old run down prison, the place is supposedly very haunted. It made the Travel Channel's *101 Things to Do Before You Die* and *Scariest Places on Earth*. You also may have seen the reformatory in the movies. The most famous filmed here were *Air Force One* and *The Shawshank Redemption*. So who knows what tales (or tails) I will bring back this time in an old musty dudgeon-like prison where brutality was common.

We will be leaving early for Mansfield to check out the city before our prison stay. Years ago dad took the family on a few day trips to Mansfield and brought us to see Kingswood Center Gardens. I thought, since we will be there, why not for memories sake see it again. Another place he took us to was a park that honored Johnny Appleseed. He lived in the area at one time. It will be interesting to see if I can find it.

Take Off

We were supposed to drive the Go-Go Bus, but a mysterious ailment cropped up right before leaving. The main and auxiliary batteries were completely drained and the alternator was shot. How do all three go bad at once? I thought it was an omen of things to come and the ghosts of Mansfield came to visit us before we went to visit them. We switched vehicles and took off.

Mansfield Arrival

I missed the exit, so took the second one a few miles down. It actually helped because it put us on the correct route for one of the places we wanted to see, Kingwood Center Gardens. Who needs GPS?

My memory did not serve me well. Kingwood was much different than the scant memories I had of it. About the only thing I remembered correctly were the greenhouse and all the flowers. Kingwood Center is a 47-acre display garden. The mansion is 22,000 square feet and was the home of Mr. King who was President and Chairman for Ohio Brass Company. The gardens and mansion are still free. It's definitely worth a visit.

We finished the Kingswood tour then found the park. My memory failed again as I remember it being out in the middle of nowhere, a forest-like park. Nope, it's right in the city. It's called the Blockhouse in South Park. The condition of it today is very run down. Sad! The monument honoring Johnny Appleseed is still there, but like the rest of the park, it's badly worn. Blockhouse is also a little different then what I remember. I thought it was more log cabin-like. On one family outing grandpa came along and read the Bible to us sitting on a picnic table in the shade of the house. It was neat to revisit it.

After a wonderful stroll through the grounds of Kingwood, enjoying God's beauty, followed by a delightful supper in Blockhouse Park reminiscing, it was time to make our way to the gloomy Mansfield Reformatory.

Prison Arrival

We continued on our way towards the edge of town and BAM, there was the reformatory! It was just an awesome, eerie sight. It sits alone and is so HUGE and GOTHIC-looking that it sent chills up our spines. It definitely gives you the willies. We couldn't believe that we were going to tour it – and in the dark! What made it even spookier is that it's right next to the new prison. I didn't know this at the time, but I took a photo of the new penitentiary. Later on our guide told us it is a state law you CANNOT TAKE ANY PHOTOS OF THE NEW PRISON, they will fine you and confiscate your camera. Whoops! Too late!

The size of the crowd for this event was about 45. Some were giggling as they were anticipating what lies beyond the huge doors. Some wore all black, some dressed in military boots and pants. Others had all kinds of equipment. Everyone on the tour had to sign a waiver. I took my turn and read CONDITIONS: I wrote, "Warm and slightly humid." SELF-CONDITIONS: I wrote again, "Warm and slightly humid." The lady looked at me as if I was whacked. Well, she didn't explain what they meant by conditions. I still don't know!

Now this is the honest truth, I don't fabricate things or lie, plus there was my sister, Jeff and the crowd to verify this. Just as Sherry the Ghost Hunter said "OK, everyone gather around and listen," a bat flew out of the main entrance to the prison and disappeared. My sister kept asking "I want to know where the bat went?" I'm telling you, a better opening script couldn't have been written. WHERE DID THAT BAT GO?

Fear Factor

The whole experience was spooky and almost dangerous, so it's high on the fear factor scale. If you like chills this is for you! Very dark, no light except what your flashlight gives off. Climbing stairs, in and out of cells, even death row was open for us to tour. The place is so large that we only ran into a few from our group. Then your mind wanders and wonders, "Suppose there is a psycho amongst us, hiding, waiting for a victim? Or ghost or ghoul?" You never know!

Ghosts or No Ghosts

So I am sure you'll want to know if we saw any ghosts. Should I jump ahead and tell you? I guess I should. Nope! OK, I know it's kind of anti-climactic now, but the rest still makes good reading. Well, you know what? In a way we did see a ghostly figure.

Our guide gave us a very brief tour of the prison, just enough for us to understand the lay out. In the rooms she did take us in, she gave a short talk of what the rooms were used for and what went on in them. The shower room was on this list. The guide insisted a ghost that she named "Mr. Anderson" appears and answers questions, but only here in the shower room. She then went on to give a demonstration on how to use divining rods to locate ghosts and spirits. She asked Mr. Anderson "Are you in the room?" The one rod swung to her left. I watched intently her fingers and did not see her roll them to move the rod. Was it a trick or did a spirit actually move the rods? I don't know. She asked him a few more questions and supposedly he didn't answer, so the rods didn't move. Then she added, "If you hold them over most people's heads, the rods will move." As a demonstration she held them over Jeff's head and the rods crossed. Just as the rods moved a lady snapped a photo. In this photo over Jeff's head you can see a hazy figure. The lady's camera was passed around and all of us saw it. So yes, we did see a ghost, but only in a photo taken of Jeff.

About the Prison

Now about those showers; this is gross. The prisoners were allowed one shower every Saturday and only had one minute to take it. That's punishment enough. Then I asked what did they use for toilets in the early years? Each cell had a pot and the last man in the cell at night had to empty it in the morning. Can you imagine 1,300 prisoners in a place with no air, very cramped cells and a 60-second shower once a week? Then can you imagine each cell with a full pot? Do you know what the place must have smelled like? If there is a ghost from the early years lurking around, his name would have to be "Gasper!"

Religion in Prison

This segment is about religion and the churches in the reformatory. Yes churches, it had two! The reformatory was grandly and elegantly built in the belief it would help sway the incarcerated back to the straight and narrow. In the early years it was mostly Protestant so it had only one church. As the years went by and the beliefs of the incoming inmates changed another church was added, a Catholic church.

The Protestant church is ONE HUGE ROOM! In fact, it could stand alone as a church. It has a HIGH ceiling and early on it had a balcony for the choir. Time has taken its toll on it; very little is left, just a few pews and a few panels of stained glass windows showing the way of the cross. It must have been a sight to see in the early years. Many years later it was converted a few times for different purposes, one was a game room. I found it amazing how religion played a part in trying to reform the prisoners, and then later on as the prisoners became more hardened, church was abandoned in favor of games.

A chaplain was also always on duty for counseling; later on, however, I am not sure. Even though church and religion were not as promoted as in the beginning, you can still find in many of the cells religious reading material left behind: Bibles, booklets and books. The other thing you find a lot of in the prison cells is empty cigarette packs. And if you put the religious materials together with cigarettes, you know what you get, don't you? Well, you get a Holy Smoke!

Never Pass an Oportunity
To Expand Your Horizons

Chapter Eighteen

Pace Yourself

I was visiting Clifton Gorge for a third time to show Walt and Jimmy the fantastic scenery. We hiked a short distance and Jimmy had seen enough, he was hungry and ready to eat.

So Walt said "I'll tell you what, next scenic overlook we'll turn around." Jimmy said "What about 100 paces more?" Walt said "OK, but as long as they are normal paces and not baby steps." I questioned this plan with "What happens if we are only three paces away from the overlook, does that mean we can't see it?"

Jimmy started the countdown: "one pace, two paces, three paces...10...25...50...75...95 paces.

Just then around the bend a group of four hikers crossed our path and one, kind of excited and out of breath, noticed our cameras and said "Thirty paces to the left is a goose on a ledge that would make an excellent photo." He pointed and we laughed. I am sure as he walked away he had to ask himself what was so funny about a goose on a ledge?

Jimmy reluctantly started the count over: one pace, two paces ......and exactly at 30 paces, YEP! THERE'S THE GOOSE ON THE LEDGE!

Chapter Nineteen

Morning Revenge

My friend and I arrived at our campsite way past midnight. We had to set up and didn't eat yet, so we had to do both, but as quietly as possible because noise travels at night.

Unloading our gear and putting up our tent wasn't too bad, but the chopping of the wood, well, it did kind of echo as did the repeated closing of my van doors. We finished our chores of setting up camp and had our late night meal about 2:00 a.m. We then headed to our tents. I was content I ate and no one yelled at us to be quiet. I crawled into my sleeping bag all comfy ready to get a good night's sleep.

About 6:30 a.m. there was such a loud ruckus; it made me jump. I heard kids yelling and what sounded like cymbals. I peeked out and saw children running around our campsite banging on pots and pans yelling, and I mean yelling "WAKE UP! WAKE UP! WAKE UP!" I was horrified!

The children circled our campsite at least three times, maybe more. I thought for sure they would drag us out of our tents. Thank God they didn't, but they definitely got revenge because I never did fall back to sleep.

Chapter Twenty

Notes from the Trip to
Butcher Holler, Kentucky

The trip to Butcher Holler, Kentucky was set up by Nancy; it was a trip with a lot of fun. Butcher Holler is the birthplace of country singers Loretta Lynn and Crystal Gayle. We took a tour of Loretta Lynn's house and grounds and met Herman, Loretta's brother, and Madonna, her niece. I just love rags to riches stories – and this is definitely one of them!

We also toured the Coal Miner's Museum of Van Lear. We were going to tour the museum first, but it was getting late so the tour guide, Tina Webb, told us to go ahead to Butchers Holler, see that and then come back. Sure enough, Tina waited for us and gave a personal tour after hours. How many volunteers do you know who would go that far?

The best, unexpected treat was the free Bluegrass festival in West Liberty that we stumbled upon. Talk about great timing! It is held annually at the Old Mill Park. What's even better than that was running into Rodney Dillard. I met Rodney the first time in Branson, Missouri at Jim Bakker's Studio City Cafe. We talked like old friends. I asked how Jim Bakker was doing and Rodney told me a few stories about him that you will never hear from the mainstream media. One was how humble Jim really is and the other was how he opened numerous hospitals in Europe.

Unfortunately I handed Lori, who came along on the trip, the video camera. After my conversation with Rodney ended I turned to her and said "You can turn the cam off." She replied, "OH, you wanted me to record you?" I'm still upset about that one!

Another interesting person we met was Don Clark who runs The Bluegrass Bus Museum. His son loved my Go-Go Bus T-shirt so we swapped shirts. I got a Martha White Flour/Bluegrass Bus Museum T-shirt and he got a Go-Go Bus T-shirt. I was informed that, at one time, Martha White Flour sponsored the early Bluegrass radio shows.

After the festival we started our trek back home. We could have taken interstate Rt. 64, but instead chose Rt. 60. This was the main route before Interstate Rt. 64 was constructed, but now Rt. 60 has become a secondary road. It is much more laid back and scenic.

Here's an eating tip: If you are ever on Rt. 60 and passing through Culloden, West Virginia, you must stop at Hillbilly Hot Dogs. Their slogan is "We got the weenies," and they sure do! It's just a terrific place to eat. They have a three-pound hotdog, and if you can eat it, it's free. I asked "Besides it being free if you eat it, is the ride in the ambulance also free?" I don't see how anyone could eat a hotdog that big. Oh, and if you are lucky, they may even break out and sing their hotdog song.

Later on while still in West Virginia we stopped at a roadside rest stop. I spotted a little Daewoo Lanos like the one I drive, which is not that common of a car. I walked around it trying to figure out which person at the rest area owned it. After a few minutes a guy walked up and said "It's a Daewoo." His name was Mr. Pray. How's that for a last name? We talked at length and he told me he was, amongst many other things, a motivational speaker. No kidding! His personality was so upbeat I could listen to this guy for hours. He gave me something that made me feel like...well, like a close friend. He gave me a CD with photos of his 50th class reunion, which he only made enough for his friends. Mr. Pray added, "Now you can see what black people do at their reunions." How funny!

Chapter Twenty-One

Greenville and the
Tionesta Breakdown

I've Been Asked, "Does the
Go-Go Bus Always Breakdown?"

Well, yeah, in a way! I am sure you have noticed this occurrence in a few stories. The best part of nostalgia is you only remember the good. When older vehicles run right they are so much better to drive than newer vehicles in my opinion. But the older ones do end up on the side of the road way more often than newer vehicles. People forget this. You never know when your classic cruiser might cough and stall because most older cars of yesteryear only had idiot lights, no gauges or "check engine" soon warnings, and usually those idiot lights went off right before disaster struck. So driving an old vehicle is an adventure and driving miles from home is an even bigger adventure. That's why I tell people I carry a mailbox on a post. If I breakdown and can't get help, I just plant it and claim squatting rights. After all, the Go-Go Bus does have everything I need – including a kitchen sink. Here is a story of when I almost planted that mailbox.

I have a saying whenever I have a destination to get to that goes like this: "I don't care how we get there as long as we get there; I'll worry how to get back once we get there." Well I had to worry how to get back from the trip to Greenville, Pennsylvania.

The night before embarking for Greenville I drove the Go-Go Bus to fill her up with gas. Right after that the Go-Go Bus went dim; it stalled and wouldn't start. Right at a busy intersection it sat. Thank God for the road crew painting stripes on the roads! They saw me sitting with cars behind blowing their horns.

The first worker comes over, and instead of asking if something is wrong, he says "Wow! Is this vehicle cool! What is it?" Another worker runs up to take a look inside. I needed to remind them "HEY! We're in the middle of the road, my battery died!" They said "Well, let us help." They pushed it to the parking lot of Taco Bell. I thought I was saved by the Bell but I wasn't. In the bus was my battery charger/starter. I asked the manager if I could plug in my starter to jump my vehicle. "NO! NO!" And with that he quickly shut the door. WOW! Gotta love corporate America! So AAA came to the rescue. They jumped the Go-Go Bus and I made it home.

The next morning it started right up, but the auxiliary battery wouldn't hold a charge, so I dropped in a spare battery. This is where a huge blunder took place that would rear its ugly head on the trip. Because of this mistake the trip literally started off with a bang. No, make that a bang and a BANG!

In my haste to leave, the positive cable on the auxiliary battery wasn't tightened. I found this out a little past Chardon on Rt. 322 when it came loose and touched the metal box the battery is housed in. The sound was so loud it sounded like a backfire and the second time was even louder. Mike, who was sitting at the table, yelled "There is smoke back here!" I pulled off the road to check on things. The electronic boxes for my florescent lights literally exploded. I reconnected the positive cable and off we went. Unfortunately, the ammeter was reading a little below half and the volts were also down. Of course I didn't let on to Ruth or Mike what the gauges were reading. I was determined to get to our destination, Greenville, and I did.

Greenville was kind of spooky at night, especially driving though the alleys. I flagged down a cop to ask if there was a place in town we could park and sleep for the night. After some questioning and shining his light in our eyes, he told us where we could stay, Riverside Park. He would inform his partner and both would check on us. "But just don't go running around!" With that warning he left.

Mike was a bit nerved on the way to Riverside Park when we approached a graveyard and said "I am not staying by a cemetery." I added to his apprehension by replying "Remember *Night of the Living Dead?* Well that was filmed in a cemetery and in Pennsylvania?" The park was further down so those fears were laid to rest. Too bad I didn't rest. I had a horrible night of sleep. Sometimes insomnia just hits me, and the noise from the trains that rumbled through kept my eyes open. They were so loud that it didn't even wake Ruth or Mike. Then about daybreak cars started pulling in with people running every which way. I thought maybe the graves did burst open and this was *Dawn of the Living Dead*. We found out later it was the registration and lineup for the Heritage Days 5K Run.

Since all that noise and commotion woke me, I for once was early, the 31st to register my vehicle for the Heritage Days car show, the reason for the trip to Greenville. Bill, the organizer and promoter of the event, said there will be some Griswolds who have to show up early. I was one of the Griswolds. A volunteer that was helping park cars when he saw the Go-Go Bus came up to me and said "I heard you arrived at 2:30 a.m." At the registration table someone again remarked "We heard you arrived at 2:30 a.m."

After getting registered and parked we ate breakfast at a family restaurant, then waited for the car show to gather steam. At first it was slow and I thought maybe I wasted my time by driving all this way, but then WHAM! It got crazy busy. The official count of registered vehicles for the Greenville Heritage Days car show was 497. The estimated number was about 600 in attendance because many do not register, they just show up. Most stores in town stay open, so besides looking at cars you can browse the shops, which was fun. We really enjoyed this show; it was an event to attend.

During the show I sat at the table inside of the Go-Go Bus, greeting people and promoting my book. A man looks in and says "So you arrived at 2:30 a.m. huh." "How did you know?" "Well I know everything that goes on around here; I am the ex-chief of police." His name was Barry. No matter where I went I kept running into him. One encounter I asked for a place to eat. He directed us to his daughter's restaurant, Steph's Corner Pub & Grille on Main Street. Mike wanted to cool off in Steph's, and I wanted to eat in the Go-Go Bus. Mike swayed us by saying he would pay. So Mike and Ruth stayed put while I ran back and forth between the bus and pub. Every time I ran back I sold a book.

The food at Steph's was very good. After lunch I ran into Barry yet again and jokingly told him "Alright, we ate at your restaurant, so you could quit following us now."

When we returned to the Go-Go Bus, sitting in my chair was Vince of Hermitage. I met Vince back in 2004 at a W. Bush Rally. Years later Jeb Bush is running for president and I see him again. We had a great time catching up, laughing and greeting people looking at the Go-Go Bus. As Vince was leaving I said "Hope to see you again before another Bush runs!"

What I found amazing was the amount of people who kept talking politics and religion to me at the show. I don't mind at all, but when I am at a fun event, not many serious topics are discussed. It's fun talk, car-related talk, or small talk! One elderly gentleman gave me his whole life story. He was married and a bad drunk. His wife left him so he had to raise his son alone. Before taking off for work one day he told his son to make sure he showers and is ready when he comes home so they can go out to dinner. When the man arrived home close to dusk, his son was outside and not ready. He was mad until the son said "Dad I can't see inside." Their lights were turned off for failure to pay the electric bill. Right then the man looked up and said "God, if you're real, help me!" He went to AA, restored his life and never drank again.

The same man more recently had an emergency doctor's appointment to fix an aneurysm in his heart. He told God "I don't have time for this, I want to go hunting." The following day he arrives for the operation, but pre-op X-rays showed nothing. Doctors compared the first X-rays to the current ones and it was no longer there. The man carries them around to show people. Hey, I am just repeating what was told to me!

The car show was also productive for selling my book. Two stores decided to carry it. What was fascinating about one of the shops was the owner's name. Her name is Reda Carey. I said loudly "Carey is your last name? What kind of a last name is that? My first name is Carey. I think my book was made for this store!" Reda agreed.

Before heading out for new horizons we stuck around for the wine give away. During the second round I won a bottle of "Gear Bang'in Grape" from Freedom Run Winery of Lockport, New York. Now the real fun was about to begin, um, not from drinking, but well...read on!

Our options were an invite to nearby Hermitage, Pennsylvania to dine with Vince and his friends, head back to Ohio for the antique steam engine show in Williamsfield and join my friend Dave, or drive further into Pennsylvania and visit Tionesta. We decided on Tionesta.

The drive from Greenville to Tionesta had us pass through Sandy Lake (No BOOM this time. Read my first book, you'll understand.), Franklin, and Oil City. Franklin looked like a neat town but we only stopped at the Shop 'n Save. I was quite amused at the checkout counter when three giggling preteen girls came in laughing. As I approached the register the clerk working it asked "Is that your vehicle everyone is talking about?" I said "It is." "Well, when I'm done with you I am shutting my register so I can go look at it. Do you mind?" The girls heard this, so they followed us. Two of the girls got in and made themselves at home when the third standing outside loudly said "HEY, do you realize you are in this man's van that you don't even know." Just funny!

After passing through scenic Oil City, which was completely dead on the 4th of July, we arrived in Tionesta, a sleepy little town of about 500. It was a long day, so no sightseeing, straight to the campground. On the edge of town are two campgrounds which I believe are state-run. The one to the right is $30 per night and developed, the one to the left is $15 per night but no electricity and no pads to park on. Of course, we went the $15 route.

Pulling in to anyplace is always fun with the Go-Go Bus. I park and immediately the next campsite over came to see what the heck I was driving. Then I had a Ranger stop by who wouldn't leave. Just like in the Greenville car show the Ranger stopped by to look at what I was driving, but then our talk drifted towards politics, morals in America, conspiracies, and religion. I hated to shoo him away because I sensed he wanted to gab some more and pick my brain, but our stomachs were calling; it was time to start a fire for supper.

I grabbed some dried needles under a pine tree. I found a dried branch in the river (Yes, it's possible!), crumpled up some newspapers and then I cheated. The Go-Go Bus is a hard starter so starting fluid is always carried. I used it to get the fire going. I really don't recommend making a fire this way as the can could ignite and explode, but it does work. A camper to the right of us saw this so he came over and plopped down a small pile of kindling. Not to be outdone, another camper came over with some decent-sized logs for the fire. What a blessing! The fire was blazing in no time. We ate supper, took a short night hike and then to bed early as we wanted to hit the road as soon as we woke.

In the morning the bus started right up with no problems. (Please note that statement.) Since it was Sunday and still relatively early, all of us agreed attending church would be nice. The first church we passed had started already but the second church, Tionesta Presbyterian Church, on the corner of Elm and Church Street hadn't, so that's where we went. I enjoyed the service, fairly traditional with an organist and hymn books.

When the service was over two elderly ladies turned and greeted us, their names were Shirley and Pat. Shirley asked "Where are you going to eat?" I replied "Your place." She in turn replied "Well I hope you like bacon and eggs because that's all I got." "Perfect," I replied. "That's Mike's favorite." Shirley looked a bit worried and nervously said "I was only joking... weren't you?" "Nope, I was serious." "OK, I guess, but let me run home first to get a few things ready." Pat, the other lady, jumped in and said "Leave your vehicle parked and I will drive the three of you to

Shirley's." "That's fine with me." Before leaving for our lunch we were given a complete tour of the church and shown how the movable wall functions. Everyone needs to see that!

Pat drove us to Shirley's as she said, but instead of going straight there she decided to take us on a short walk to see the Forest County Court House and a war memorial. For an elderly lady she was so spry; we worked to keep up with her on our walk. We then went to Shirley's. Prepared for us was such a wonderful lunch, and her hospitality was even better! Our lunch consisted of homemade bread and strawberry jelly, raspberry jam, pan-cakes, bacon, eggs, and coffee. We spent most of the afternoon there just talking away and really enjoying ourselves on her patio. At 4:00 p.m. it was time to get moving. Hugs and "thank you's" were given and off we went. What terrific Godly people! We were blessed!

Even though I wrote Tionesta is a sleepy town, it does have things to do and see. There is the Tionesta Market Village. Their website reads "The Tionesta Market Village is a unique artisan shopping experience located on the edge on the Allegheny National Forest, right in the heart of downtown Tionesta, Penn-sylvania." "Right in the heart of downtown" gave me a chuckle. I guess it is a "downtown," but the size of it, well.....there is also the Sherman Memorial Lighthouse, the Tionesta Indian Festival held in August (which has nothing to do with native American Indians), and of course Tionesta Lake. The Tionesta Lake area is one of the best big game regions in Pennsylvania.

We finally made it back to the Go-Go Bus, slammed the doors, turned the key and – and – and nothing. Mike thought I was joking. No joke, the battery was dead. Now what! Mike suggested he would walk over to the store we were just at and ask someone what to do. Without even asking my thoughts, Mike called Frank's Towing. That was mistake number one unless you count the mistake at the beginning of the trip with the battery, then this would be mistake number two. We went back and forth and whether we should cancel the tow because I had AAA. While discussing our plight Frank's pulls up. He takes AAA. After a quick testing of the Go-Go Bus Steve of Frank's Towing tells me the bad news, "Alternator, you're not charging."

I told Steve we cannot be stuck here; Mike and I both have to work tomorrow. So I called Auto Zone for an alternator, but it was the one in Conneaut, Pennsylvania, which is located many miles away from where we were at. I was looking for Warren, Pennsylvania, which is a manageable distance of 40 miles or so. After a few more calls to Auto Zone (that kept connecting us back to Conneaut), the last call finally went to Warren. While this fiasco is happening we hear the tow truck driver Steve talk on his phone saying he would hurry up on this call so he could meet for supper. Another mistake was made for not putting Steve's phone conversation together with the advice he was about to give us. Anyway, back to Auto Zone in Warren, the worker gave me directions to his store. I was completely lost. I handed the phone to Steve the tow driver. He was equally as confused until he asked "Where are you?" "We are north of Detroit." What the heck! We were talking to Warren, Michigan not Warren, Pennsylvania!

Time was now waning as it was fast approaching 6:00 p.m. But I was insistent on not giving up on finding an alternator. Steve the tow driver with plans of his own and not wanting to be delayed kept repeating "YOU are in a small town with nothing around on a Sunday night, you are not going anywhere." "But if I can get to Warren..." "YOU are in a small town with nothing around on a Sunday night, you are not going anywhere." "Yes, but the..." "YOU are in a small town with nothing around on a Sunday night, you are not going anywhere. Besides, I can't tow something this large, your vehicle is too big." We found out later that last statement was nothing but a lie and deception. Steve went on to say "Listen, you can spend all your money or I can give you a jump so you can drive to the Mid-Town Motel where you can strike up a deal with Adam the owner, and in the morning go across the street to the Greathouse Body Shop and have it fixed." So Steve got us started and we drove three blocks down the street to the parking lot of the Mid-Town. He followed behind then quickly took off for his supper date.

Mike was now nearing meltdown or boil-over, or maybe both at the same time. "I CANNOT BE STUCK HERE, I HAVE TO WORK, I CANNOT BE STUCK HERE." Now I had the added stress of calming Mike down. I couldn't think straight. So I said "Please go, you and Ruth take a walk, go buy us some spaghetti and sauce and I will cook." And that's what they did.

Meanwhile, not being deterred I called O'Reilly's in Warren, Pennsylvania, not Michigan. Success, I have them on the first call. Unfortunately they do not have my alternator. "OK, where is the nearest one?" "A place called...umm...Eastlake, Ohio." "EASTLAKE! That is one suburb over from where I live!" Unbelievable! Mike and Ruth arrived back with the food supplies. I made pasta right in the parking lot. But a full stomach didn't work. Mike was starting to really come unhinged, unraveled, unstable and nuclear. "Mike, what am I supposed to do? We are in a small town with nothing around on a Sunday night, we are not going anywhere." All Mike could say was "ERRRR, AHHHH, GROWLLLL!"

Then it occurred to me, PAUL, call Paul. "Hello Paul, I'm stuck, uh, it's a little far, Tionesta, Pennsylvania." Long pause. "But first you need to pick up my alternator." Another pause! "Excellent, thank you, thank you." Paul's coming, we're saved. Mike decided to get a motel room, this way he could relax and take a nap while we waited for Paul. It was now dark and I myself was under the bus busy removing the alternator with a flashlight. As I am working on it the same ranger from the campground came over and called me by my name and asked "Carey, what's up?" It made me feel good that a patrolman remembered my name for a good reason and not to give me a ticket. I was also thankful he stopped to check on me and not talk politics. With the alternator now off and waiting for Paul, Ruth and I took a walk through town. It's quiet during the day and even more so at night. The only sound was our feet and an occasional vehicle that passed. It was eerie fun.

Hours later Paul finally arrives with the alternator. So our troubles are solved, right? Nope! It was the wrong alternator. We are now officially stuck. Mike leaves his boss another update, calls off work, and succumbs to the fact that we are in a small town with nothing around on a Sunday night, we are not going anywhere, and falls asleep for the night in the motel. I leave the alternator across the street at Greathouse Body Shop with a note explaining to swap the pulleys on the alternators, the new one has a two-groove pulley, the old one has a one groove pulley.

We woke relatively early and across the street I went to Greathouse inquiring if the alternator was fixed. "Oh no, I had cars in front of you, what did you need done?" Oh boy! I explain and he says "I can't swap pulleys, but there is a shop nearby that can." Another delay, and Mike with a good rest had renewed energy to panic yet again. "I NEED TO GET OUT OF HERE NOW, PAUL LETS GO!" Paul was not about to abandon us, so it was his turn to quiet Mike. Finally about noon Greathouse calls me over, the shop did the necessary pulley swap and the alternator is done. I crawl under the bus and put the alternator on in record time. The Go-Go Bus fired right up; the gauges though read a different story, still not quite up to snuff. Once more I ignore them. We had to get out of this town. It's 16 miles to Titusville, then another 115 miles home. I am sure I can limp the bus home.

As we approached Titusville the Go-Go Bus started chugging. The alternator wasn't charging. It let out one horrendously loud backfire, which shook Ruth who thought it was exploding. BANG! It died right on the edge of town. Now what? The only thing left is the voltage regulator. I was thankful Paul didn't split because he drove us through town looking for a parts store. We found Advance Auto Parts and what did they say? "Sure, we have your regulator, but it won't be here until afternoon around three." I now had the unfortunate task of informing Mike we had to kill another couple of hours. So what to do? First we ate and then we went sightseeing and drove around Woodlawn Cemetery. I thought it was scenic, but I don't think Mike did and may even have been picking out my plot if we didn't get back. After the graveyard tour we had to waste more time, so we visited a grocery store to pick up snacks, then on to Advance Auto Parts.

Finally I had the new regulator in hand! What could possibly go wrong? Paul drove us back to the bus and I quickly installed it. And guess what? It didn't charge. Unbelievable! So I made another call to AAA. They quickly sent over someone from Shambaugh Towing who towed us to an auto repair they suggested. Unfortunately the garage was closed so I asked "Can you drive me to one that is open?" Suddenly they received an emergency call. Whether I liked it or not I was unhooked and left alone.

Mike thought, "OK, we're leaving the bus, we can finally get going." Nope, not yet! I had more stones to turn over before I was satisfied that I couldn't drive home. So off we went to find an open garage. We found one but the man said "Sorry, you need to leave it. I have too many cars before yours." I reluctantly gave up that the Go-Go Bus would be left behind.

On the way back to the bus to grab a few things before heading home with Paul, I decided to call mom and check in with her since it was a few days since we spoke. I told her what was going on, and what did she say so lovingly? "What's the matter with you, you got AAA. You got 100 miles of free tow!" Wait a second, I do! Of course mom had to throw at me loudly "You always need your mother, don't you? You need your mother, uhuh, but you won't admit it, right!" "OK! OK! You're right! Bye!"

Then my mind raced backwards. If Steve of Frank's Towing would not have lied and was not in a hurry for his dinner date, we could have been towed only 30 miles short of home Sunday night. That rat! So back on the phone with AAA and back came a Schambaugh tow truck driver. And unlike Frank's Towing, Schambaugh felt proud to tow the Go-Go Bus. Before we left the driver snapped photos so he could brag to his friends what he got to tow. Ruth and I and the Go-Go Bus were finally on our way home. As for Mike and Paul, the minute they found out what mom said they zoomed off in a hurry.

So is this the end of the saga of the no go Go-Go Bus. Far from it! You wouldn't believe it, then again you may but I won't write about it here. Ask me sometime in person, or who knows, maybe it could make book three. BOOK THREE? Yeah – maybe!

Embrace Today
Where the Memories of Tomorrow Are Made

In Closing!

Hey Gang,

My editor once again took scissors and yelled "Cut!"

So, could there really be a book three? Yeah – well, maybe! There are still plenty of road tales to tell lying on the cutting room floor.

Besides, many of you have asked "Am I in it" when referring to the books I have written, and then proceed to recall a road trip or adventure we experienced together. Well, just because it may not have been put into words yet, I repeat the word "yet," I do remember the time we went... which very well could be the title of the next book.

Therefore, until I once again turn the ignition key and put ink to paper, stay packed and ready with your eyes on the road. I may be rounding the bend.

As I wrote in my previous work, if you would like to keep abreast of my adventures, just visit www.gogobus.cc whenever you have some free time.

Gotta Go-Go!
Carey Masci

Made in the USA
Lexington, KY
17 April 2018